THESE RELIGIOUS AFFECTIONS

These
Religious Affections

By
Harold John Ockenga
*Minister, Park Street Congregational Church,
Boston, Mass.*

WIPF & STOCK · Eugene, Oregon

Wipf and Stock Publishers
199 W 8th Ave, Suite 3
Eugene, OR 97401

These Religious Affections
By Ockenga, Harold John and Rosell, Garth M.
Copyright©1937 by Ockenga, Harold John
ISBN 13: 978-1-5326-1736-2
Publication date 1/25/2017
Previously published by Zondervan, 1937

To
MY EXCELLENT WIFE AND HELPMATE
IN ALL OF LIFE'S
UNDERTAKINGS

PREFACE

CHRISTIANITY has twice reached the extreme of externalism. Once this happened under the Roman Church through the adding of penance, indulgences, and works of merit to the Gospel. The masses soon identified Christianity with these external acts. The reaction against this came in the form of the Reformation, the return to a religion of the heart. Again this externalism occurred under the Protestants through emphasis upon the social gospel. By some religious thinkers God was identified with the social process. From this we are experiencing a very wholesome reaction in a return to personal Christianity. True that the emphasis is not always Biblical, as in the case of the Oxford Groups or in the case of the supra-church membership advanced by the Oxford Ecumenical Conference, but the return to Christianity, as a religion of the heart, is evident.

We hold this to be exceedingly encouraging to those who have been preaching Biblical Christianity. It may be that a new day is ahead for the only religion which is able to affect the depths of man's nature, his heart. Under the affections of the heart may be subsumed all of the fundamental attitudes of man toward the Gospel and the resultant effect of that Gospel upon his nature. By means of the Bible terms describing the heart of man we shall treat some of these facts.

This little book is merely part of a series of sermons upon this subject delivered in Park Street Congregational Church, Boston, and published at the request of the congregation for wider distribution. We send it forth with the hope that when these subjects again rise to foremost interest in men's minds—as they shall—it may help to point the way.

H. J. O.

Boston, Massachusetts.

CONTENTS

I.	THE RELIGIOUS HEART	11
II.	THE WICKED HEART	24
III.	THE PRICKED HEART	40
IV.	THE CONTRITE HEART	55
V.	THE BELIEVING HEART	71
VI.	THE HARDENED HEART	87
VII.	THE BURNING HEART	103
VIII.	THE PURE HEART	118
IX.	THE TROUBLED HEART	132
X.	THE LOVING HEART	148

I.

THE RELIGIOUS HEART

"Whom having not seen, ye love; in whom, though now ye see him not, yet believing, ye rejoice with joy unspeakable and full of glory: receiving the end of your faith, even the salvation of your souls."
—I PETER 1: 8, 9.

THE occasion for these words of St. Peter, written to the sojourners of the Dispersion scattered throughout the Roman world, was the persecution which had arisen at about A. D. 60. He was encouraging them in the midst of their trials, stating that though they were in temporary heaviness through manifold temptations, yet that the trial of their faith should bring them praise and honor and glory at the appearing of Jesus Christ who, of course, would judge them according to their deeds. Then Peter spoke of their love to Christ and of their joy in Christ in spite of the trials which they were undergoing. Hence, it is evident that true religion which is able to endure in the midst of all kinds of opposition and trial consists in true religious affections which result in the salvation of the soul. Jonathan Edwards once took this thesis as the subject of a discourse and ended by writing a book upon it which differentiated between the true and false affections as they were manifested in the great awakening which occurred under the instrumentality of George Whitefield. We are indebted to him for some of the keen analysis made of religious experience which we have used in this first discussion.

Perhaps we should begin by determining what the religious affections are. The old psychology speaks of the mind and of the heart as two faculties of the soul. The new psychology speaks of cognition, feelings and conation. Emotions are those sensory experiences varying with the knowing and wishing functions, part of which are affections. Now the affections do not have their seat in the mind. That, we identify with the understanding. One may be filled with notions and speculations about religion, and in particular about Christ, and yet not love Him or have joy in Him. The affections consist of that which inclines the will and their seat is the heart. We do not distinguish the will from the affections for the will can only move as it is affected, but the affections themselves incline the will to action. These affections may be of two kinds. They may be those which cleave to or those which repulse. In the former are included such affections as love, desire, joy, gratitude, humility and meekness, whereas in the latter are included affections such as hatred, fear, anger, dislike and pride. When these emotions are brought to bear upon the will, it is inclined to action.

True religion actually consists of fervent inclinations or affections. God insists that we be "fervent in spirit." We are told that we must love the Lord with all our heart, soul and mind. If there is not a vigor to our affections they are nothing at all. God will have nothing to do with lukewarm, lifeless inclinations. "Because thou art lukewarm, and neither cold nor hot," said Jesus, "I will spue thee out of my mouth." The Scriptures depict the religious exercises of the heart as lively and powerful. They are compared to running and wrestling and fighting. They demand the full functioning of mind and heart. It is evident that religion takes possession of the minds of men no further than the things of religion affect them. Men sometimes hear the Word of God, the message of the Gospel, the glorious perfections of God and His unspeakable love, and yet these things make no change whatever in their behaviour. They remain exactly as they were before, without any sensible alteration either in heart or practice, because they were not affected by what they heard. A man's heart must be affected before any change will be wrought in him. "Never was anyone won and brought to the throne of grace by anything he ever heard or imagined respecting his own unworthiness and his exposure to the wrath of God, nor induced to flee for refuge to Christ while his heart remained unaffected. There never was a saint recovered from a declining state in religion without having his heart affected, and there never was anything considerable brought to pass in the heart or life of any man by the things of religion until the mind was deeply affected by those things."

The Scriptures speak much of the fear of God as a great motive to godliness. They speak of hope in God and in the promises of His Word. They speak of love to God and to mankind in general. They speak of holy desire for the satisfying truths of the Spirit and they speak of holy joy as constituting an important part of true religion. Rejoicing in the Lord is constantly mentioned as a spiritual practice. As opposed to these come the hatred of sin, the indignation over evil, the fear of judgment and the similar emotions of repulsion. These are the affections, but love is always represented as the greatest motivating force of all. Love is the fulfilling of the law. Love is the manifestation of pure religion. Love is greater than faith and hope. It is supreme.

Consider the fact that religious ordinances deal with the affections. The foremost practice of religion is prayer; but prayer is not for the purpose of affecting or inclining the heart of God so much as it is to incline our hearts and the hearts of others toward the reception of the blessings for which we ask. Song in public service is used purely to excite and express the religious affections. What reason is there to worship God in verse rather than in prose and with music if it is not that our natures are affected by these things? Undoubtedly the Word of God, telling us of the doctrines of eternal truth and of the nature of Deity, is for this same purpose. God has appointed the means of preaching the Word as the instrument in affecting sinners with the importance of the things of Christianity and with the necessity of loving God. Even with the saints, the effect of preaching the Word of God is to produce a heart love and joy. The very sacraments affect us by exhibiting to our view what Christ has done in lifting the burden of the world's sin and sorrow, thereby more deeply moving us.

The Religious Heart 15

On the other hand, heart hardness is designated as the essence of sin. To this, rejection of Christ and the opposition to Christianity are distinctly ascribed. When Paul saw his message was rejected by the Jews he spoke of their being hardened. In fact, the prophet Isaiah and also Ezekiel attributed hardness of heart to the Jews. Whenever men are left to the power of their depravity and sin, they are spoken of as having their hearts hardened. So it was with the Pharisees with whom Jesus dealt, and with Nebuchadnezzar, who stiffened his neck and hardened his heart, and with the Pharaoh of the Exodus who rejected the message of Moses. Conversion is spoken of as consisting in the taking away of a heart of stone and the substituting for it of the heart of flesh. Listen to Ezekiel: "I will give them one heart, and I will put a new spirit within you; and I will take the stony heart out of their flesh, and I will give them a heart of flesh." Thus it is evident that the presence or absence of true religion is designated by the condition of the heart.

Since a hard heart is one destitute of pious affections what may we learn which will stimulate our religious affections, our holy emotions? What truths are there which are able to permeate the whole of our nature rather than remain isolated in a cold, intellectual conception of the mind? Perhaps we may learn by considering: first, the source of a religious heart; second, the manifestations of a religious heart; and third, the fruit of a religious heart, all of which we shall have only a brief moment to mention and which later we expect to examine through the great experiences of characters of the Scriptures.

I. THE SOURCE OF A RELIGIOUS HEART.

The source of true religious affections is the gracious, supernatural influence of the Holy Spirit in the life of the individual. The New Testament differentiates between a spiritual person and a natural person. Says Paul, "The natural man receiveth not the things of the Spirit of God: for they are foolishness unto him: neither can he know them, because they are spiritually discerned. But he that is spiritual judgeth all things." The natural man according to the New Testament is an ungodly man. He is one who is devoid of other than common influences of the Spirit. Natural men, regardless of their gifts, are never called spiritual. They are not recipients of any of those effects, gifts or qualities which are derived directly from the Spirit of God. A spiritual man is one who has the Holy Spirit abiding in him, becoming a fountain of the water of the soul springing up unto everlasting life. And a spiritual man is also one to whom God has communicated something of His own proper nature. Saints become the temples of the living God. They partake of His moral beauty, of the holiness of His nature and of His fullness. The means of this, according to the Scripture, is regeneration, variously called the "new birth" or "being born of the Spirit" or "being renewed in mind." Ungodly men obviously are not partakers of this new nature and thus they know nothing of real grace and of that spiritual principle which is incon-

The Religious Heart 17

sistent with the state of sin. This new spiritual sense is not a new function of the understanding, but it is a new foundation laid for cognition in a condition of the heart or of the whole nature of man which has been changed. This new principle which has wrought the change is distinctly supernatural.

The Holy Spirit witnesses to the life of such a believer that he is the child of God. This witness is an assurance of the gift of grace and of being a partaker of the Divine nature. It is a confidence which arises out of the change which occurs in one's life. Paul speaks of it as the seal of the Spirit which is a token that the seal of the King of heaven is stamped upon a heart and that a moral holiness has been communicated to the individual. To this corresponds the promise in the book of Revelation, "To him that overcometh will I give to eat of the hidden manna, and will give him a white stone, and in the stone a new name written, which no man knoweth saving he that receiveth it." That witness is a moral image and likeness; as Jesus affirmed that the works which He did bore witness that the Father had sent Him, so the works of the individual bear witness of his change of nature.

This presence of the Spirit is called an earnest, that is, it is a foretaste of the heavenly fullness. Hearken to the Scriptures: "Who hath also sealed us, and given the earnest of the Spirit in our hearts," and "in whom also, after that ye believed, ye were sealed with that Holy Spirit of promise, which is the earnest of our inheritance until the redemption of a purchased possession, unto the praise of His glory." An earnest was a present payment of money to insure the future payment of the whole upon a purchase. The Spirit of God is a present gift as a promise of our future inheritance. This is synonymous with grace or the beginning of eternal life in the soul. It is not manifested in any extraordinary gifts, but in the vital indwelling of the Spirit in the heart communicating His own nature, from whence believers draw their life, light, love, joy and holiness. We know that "As many as are led by the Spirit of God they are the sons of God; for ye have not received the spirit of adoption, whereby we cry, Abba, Father; the Spirit itself beareth witness with our spirit that we are the children of God."

II. Manifestations or Evidences of a True Religious Heart.

The first manifestation of the religious heart is an enlightenment of the mind. Holy affections invariably arise from some information conveyed to the mind from the proper view of Divine things. We are led to know more about God; as John says, "Every one that loveth is born of God and knoweth God." Our zeal is based upon knowledge. Paul says: "I pray that your love may abound yet more and more in knowledge and in all judgment." Any affections which arise from other than light in the understanding cannot be spiritual. Let us remember that our Gospel is something that may be understood. "If our gospel be hid," says Paul, "it is hid to them that are lost: in whom the god of this world hath blinded the minds of them which believe not, lest the light of the glorious gospel of Christ who is the image of God should shine unto them." Thus we see the appropriateness of the figure of conversion as an opening of the eyes of the blind. Those who are destitute of spiritual perception are spoken of as totally blind. Our affections of unspeakable joy in Christ and of love to Christ, must be based upon a knowledge which is communicated through the Divine revelation in the Scriptures.

Another manifestation of true religious affection is a conviction of the truth of the Gospel. Those who are truly regenerate no longer halt between two opinions with reference to the truth of the Christian religion. Their conviction is effectual. The doctrines of the Scriptures respecting the eternal purpose of God and His designs respecting the fall of man and the things prepared for the saints have a powerful influence upon their minds. Listen to the certainty which Peter had concerning Christ: "Thou hast the words of eternal life," he says, "And we believe and are sure that thou art that Christ, the Son of the living God." True faith "is the substance of things hoped for, the evidence of things not seen." Now the affections arise from this strong persuasion of the truth of the Christian religion. They are not merely affections which grow out of teaching, but those which arise from a rational conviction which is spiritual and which is peculiar to those who are regenerated and have the Spirit of God dwelling within them. Thus the sense of permanency and certainty of these spiritual things produces the sense of confidence and joy in the individuals.

A third manifestation of true religion is the presence of humility. There are those who feign humility, believing that it is an attribute of the Christian life. They speak of their own weakness and unworthiness and unrighteousness in order that they may appear to have humility unto men. This is a form of self-righteousness. True humility is a result of God's grace whereby we realize the depravity of our own lives and the depth of our sin against an infinitely holy God. Any righteousness of ours is as nothing in comparison with God and His demands of us. True humility is never horizontal—that is, it has nothing to do with comparisons between one's self and others as to attainments in religion. It is vertical and results from the fact that however high our attainments in morality they still appear as deformities in the light of the Divine moral viewpoint. Love, meekness and gratitude may be found most in those saints who are walking closest to the Lord. The Christian love to God and to man is a humble love; and joy, even when it is unspeakable and full of glory, is a humble joy.

Another manifestation of true religion is the change wrought in one's nature. The Scriptures abound with texts speaking of this change. Paul says, "We all, with open face beholding as in a glass the glory of the Lord, are changed into the same image from glory to glory, even as by the Spirit of the Lord." He urges the Romans to be "transformed by the renewing of their minds." And John says, "And of His fulness have all received, and grace for grace." The truly Christian, converted, regenerated, spiritual individual, is one whose nature manifests in a limited way the graces which Christ manifested upon earth. If there is no change which is abiding in persons who profess conversion there is a probability that they are deceived. Unless something which is unselfish and pure and upright begins to appear in the character of an individual, his profession may hardly be esteemed to be consistent. It is true that a man after his conversion may be in danger of falling before a particular sin or temptation to which he was inclined before his conversion; but it will not have dominion over him, for the spiritual principle which is opposed to such sin abides in him. The life of the believer, however, should take on something of that process of continued conversion where he is more and more transformed into the image of God.

The last evidence we shall mention of a true religious experience is that of a tender spirit. David says, "A broken and a contrite heart, O God, thou wilt not despise." The promise is that our heart of stone shall be turned to a heart of flesh. The conscience of a true Christian will be tender, and susceptible to godly sorrow over his shortcomings and his sins. It should be easily convicted. This, too, is a means of joy. "Serve the Lord with fear, and rejoice with trembling," says the Psalmist. And again, "The Lord taketh pleasure in them that fear him, in those that hope in his mercy." The more there is of this tender hope and joy, the more is true Christian confidence promoted.

III. FRUIT OF A TRUE RELIGIOUS HEART.

True religion must be of a practical nature and if

the affections are the essence of true religion, then they become the springs of action. The psychologists list what they call the springs of human action and they include all of our emotions. If we would take away all love and hatred, all hope and fear, all zeal and affectionate desires, the world, in a great measure, would be lifeless. Let those springs be sanctified by a true Christian experience and the practical effect on men's lives will be great. Jonathan Edwards claimed that Christian practice implies three things: first, a behaviour of conduct universally agreeing with the will of God; second, a holy conduct pursued with the greatest earnestness and diligence; and third, a perseverance in holiness to the end of life. These three things are certainly taught in the Scriptures. John says: "Every man that hath this hope in him purifieth himself even as he is pure"; and he adds, "Whosoever abideth in him sinneth not: whosoever sinneth hath not see him, neither knoweth him." The Scriptures give evidence that the Christian religion should be the main business of our life. Jesus declared that no man can serve two masters at once. Those who are the true servants of God must give themselves up to His work as the paramount occupation of their lives. Christian practice is the great and distinguishing fruit of saving grace. "By their fruits ye shall know them," says Jesus. That He emphasized the importance of this even as an evidence to others is plain enough, since He adds, "Let your light so shine before men that they may see your good works and glorify your Father which is in heaven."

Actions will test the sincerity of our profession.

The Religious Heart

While men are left to follow their own choice, they show by their actions what they prefer in their hearts. It is absurd for any one of us to say that he has a good heart while he lives a wicked life. We must bring forth the fruits of the Spirit. The Scriptures say: "By works was faith made perfect"; that is, faith is completed or evinced. "He that saith, I know Him, and keepeth not His commandments, is a liar, and the truth is not in him," John warns. "But whoso keepeth His word, in him verily is the love of God perfected."

Let us remember that it is by our deeds that we shall be judged before the judgment seat of Christ. It shall be a righteous judgment according to the conscience of every individual and it will reveal the works which we have done in the flesh. If the Lord shall use this as a criterion of judgment, so also should we. It is Christian practice which confirms true godliness. This is the most decisive proof of the saving knowledge of God. "Hereby we do know that we know Him, if we keep His commandments."

Whatever, then, will stimulate the affections as means to move the will unto holiness is desirable. Such a manner of preaching, such a mode of worshiping God in prayer, in singing praises and in testimony; such a practice as observing Holy Communion and any other method, whether it be evangelistic meetings or services for the purpose of studying the Word; whatever has a tendency to deeply affect the hearts of those who attend upon the means of grace is most desirable as a stimulant to consistent Christian action.

II.

THE WICKED HEART

"The heart is deceitful above all things and desperately wicked: who can know it?"
—Jer. 17: 9.

THE wickedness of the human heart is not a pleasant starting point for a consideration of the religious affections, but it is a very necessary one. It is imperative that we be true to those who look to us for Biblical declaration concerning the condition of human nature, just as it is obligatory upon a doctor to give his patient a true declaration of his condition. A preacher who pleases the people is as much a quack in his field as is a doctor who by comforting words lulls a diseased individual into indifference concerning his state. We cannot intelligently speak of man's affections from a Christian view without knowing what the state of man's heart is. Of course, when we use the word "heart" we are employing Bible language to deal with man's nature, which includes his intellect, his will and his affections. In order to discern the state of man we shall neither consult the psychologists nor the physicians nor the philosophers who in their fields may speak as experts, but we shall seek our answer from the Bible and that answer is abundantly plain. He who accepts the Bible will have no doubt about the condition of man's

The Wicked Heart

heart, for the Bible describes the heart of man as "evil," "wicked," "perverse," "deceitful," "despiteful," "vile," and "subtle." This is plain language. We need make no mistake about what God thinks concerning human nature.

This wickedness of the human heart constitutes the doctrine called "the depravity of man." We, together with the Presbyterians, accept the Westminster Confession of Faith as the expression of the system of doctrine contained in the Bible. The Bible teaching is a concatenated system and we must treat it as such. We are glad that this Confession is the basis of the faith of the Park Street Church, for there never was a better summary of the Bible teaching. Let me quote what the Confession says concerning the state of man.

1. Our first parents, being seduced by the subtlety and temptation of Satan, sinned in eating the forbidden fruit. This their sin God was pleased, according to His wise and holy counsel, to permit, having purposed to order it to His own glory.

2. By this sin they fell from their original righteousness, and communion with God, and so became dead in sin, and wholly defiled in all the faculties and parts of soul and body.

3. They being the root of all mankind, the guilt of this sin was imputed, and the same death in sin and corrupted nature conveyed, to all their posterity, descending from them by ordinary generation.

4. From this original corruption, whereby we are utterly indisposed, disabled, and made opposite to all

good, and wholly inclined to all evil, do proceed all actual transgressions.

5. This corruption of nature, during this life, doth remain in those that are regenerated: and although it be through Christ pardoned and mortified, yet both itself, and all the motions thereof, are truly and properly sin.

6. Every sin, both original and actual, being a transgression of the righteous law of God and contrary thereunto, doth, in its own nature bring guilt upon the sinner, whereby he is bound over to the wrath of God and curse of the law, and so made subject to death, with all misery spiritual, temporal, and eternal.

This doctrine is one of the five points of Calvinism; it is a bulwark of Bible Christianity. It is exceedingly necessary that we make it the basis of our thinking.

The wickedness of the human heart is essential to any Christian experience which we are to have through grace. To deny this condition is to deny the possibility of applying the remedy. We can never bear resemblance to the second Adam until first we have confessed our resemblance to the first Adam. Our text asks, in effect, "Who can know the depths of the iniquity of the human heart?" God alone knows this and He has told us something of it; but man himself can only know that he is wicked without knowing the intensity of that wickedness. As we read of some of the crimes which are committed in the world we are amazed that man is capable of performing them. The Bible describes a wicked heart as a "potsherd covered with silver dross," that is, it often makes a good appearance but it is nothing more than common dirt. Out of our study of the Scriptures there are several observations which we are led to make concerning the depravity of man: first, the wickedness of the heart has its origin in the Fall; second, this wickedness of the heart is the universal condition of man; and third, this wickedness of the heart leaves no help for man except in Christ.

I. THE WICKEDNESS OF THE HEART HAS ITS ORIGIN IN THE FALL.

When we speak of the Fall, we refer to the one sin out of which all others came. This Fall was the conclusion to man's period of probation. You recall that God made a covenant with man which was to last for a certain period, and if he should obey the divine command he would enter into an unending life of perfection. This does not imply that man did not already have life nor that he was imperfect. It merely states what the Bible implies when it says, "In the day thou eatest thereof thou shalt surely die." Man was good, but he was capable of evil. His goodness was not confirmed. Man had life but there was still the possibility of death. He was not established in life. Neither of these two events could take place until the period of probation had ended. That period of probation consisted of a covenant of works which demanded perfect obedience, an obedience like unto that which Jesus yielded unto God in His earthly life.

A glance at the temptation which came to man might help us to know something of the nature of the Fall. First, we must affirm that man is free either to obey

the command of God or to disobey. We cannot do away
with human freedom without blasting the responsibility
of man in this first sin. When we speak of freedom—
a free will—we do not mean that that will acts inde-
pendently of the nature of man which includes his
knowledge and his affections. It does not act inde-
pendently of his character but it is determined by these
things. Now the first man was good. He had no evil
habits or thoughts or affections to influence his choice
for evil such as all of us have had since his Fall. Why
a good man chose evil is to us an insoluble mystery,
but the Bible tells us how the evil suggestions came to
him, whence they originated and who was responsible.
Certainly it was not God. The temptation to man came
from Satan. The approach was most subtle. It was
similar to the approaches of the tempter which come
to man today. First, he held up something as desirable
which God had forbidden. He turned man's attention
to forbidden things. Then he began to question the very
fact of the command. He asked, "Hath God said?"
Surely God did not prohibit the eating from these good
trees in the garden? The woman's reply indicated that
God had commanded this, but then the tempter said, "Ye
shall *not* surely die." God had said, "Thou *shalt* surely
die," but here the tempter accused God of lying and
that for the purpose of keeping man from becoming
as He was—that is, possessing the knowledge of good
and evil. There was a bit of truth in Satan's accusation,
not that God had lied but that God did not wish man
to know the difference between good and evil by suc-

cumbing to evil. He never wishes that, although Satan's lie still is broadcast today.

I once had a schoolmate whose father was a doctor. He believed that the way to teach men the difference between good and evil was to let them experience evil, and he accompanied his own son to certain places, inducting him into the experience of sin, that he might be able to know the difference between the evil and the good. That is the lie of Satan which, when followed, blasts character. Man succumbed, and after he succumbed he knew evil and good, but he knew good only as a memory, whereas evil was his present state. He had forfeited his innocence.

Let us not think that all of this occurred outside of God's control. God embraced everything which comes to pass in His eternal plan, so that even this sin was foreknown; but God brings things to pass under different conditions and in different ways. In the sin of Adam the full responsibility of man was retained. God is not the author of sin for He neither tempts man with sin nor is He tempted with evil at any time. Yet it was God's purpose to use that evil in the history of the universe. Why He permitted man to fall must find its answer back in the eternities, in connection with the fall of the angels and the rebellion of Lucifer, the angel of the morning. The answer to that question God has not seen fit to reveal, but we know that He permitted the Fall for a holy and wise purpose.

That original sin out of which all others have come was, essentially, disobedience of God's holy law, His commands. Sin, according to the Confession and the

Bible, is still a disobedience of God's law. It has been ascribed by different thinkers to many different causes. One may define it as an anti-social practice placing its roots in custom. Another might define it as error in thinking or as an illusion of existence. Still another might identify it with matter being in conflict with spirit, but the Bible makes it clear that sin is a transgression of, or want of conformity to, God's law. Not only has every man with the exception of one confirmed this choice of Adam by deeds of his own which are violations of the law of God, thus making him evil, but he is evil and has a sense of guilt purely as a result of this first transgression of God's law. Biblical and human evidence both point to the fact that mankind is lost in sin—is wicked of heart. Though some have affirmed the contrary, we hold this to be indisputable.

The effect of the Fall on the nature of man was almost immediately made manifest. We turn a few pages in the book of Genesis and read: "And God saw that the wickedness of man was great in the earth, and that every imagination of the thoughts of his heart was only evil continually." Within a short time wickedness was the universal condition of man, demanding such a judgment as the flood. The thoughts of man's heart were such that God was ready to destroy him from the earth and to make a new beginning with a new restraining principle over man's heart, lest he exercise his imaginations to such former wickedness. This does not mean that after the Flood man's nature was changed. It is still the same, fallen and unlovely, but now it is restrained by the common influences of grace and by human gov-

The Wicked Heart

ernment. Remember that Jesus said, "If ye being evil know how to give good gifts unto your children—" He held men to be evil in heart. Is sin, then, a necessary part of human nature? To this we must answer, "No." Otherwise Jesus Christ would have been sinful for He was essentially human. How, then, shall we solve the problem of the transmission of this wickedness from one pair to all men? Perhaps all men, as some hold, were present in Adam as many oaks that came from the acorns of one oak were first present in it. This is called "Realism," but this is not substantiated by the Scriptures, since the Bible distinguishes between the souls of men. Mankind is a plurality of individuals and not merely one great all pervasive soul. Perhaps, as some hold, this sin has been transmitted by example, by the vain tradition of the elders. This would mean that each of us would have followed the example of those who went before, but surely if that were the case and we had freedom, by the law of averages some would somewhere have exercised their freedom and have lived a righteous life. How do we know that no one has? For the simple reason that the penalty which came upon Adam for his sin has been visited upon every man since Adam's day, that is, the penalty of death. The Scriptures say, "By one man's offense death reigned." That reign of death still continues. How, then, shall we answer this question? We shall answer this by the doctrine of imputation. The Catechism says, "A covenant being made with Adam, not only for himself, but for his posterity, all mankind, descending from him by ordinary generation, sinned in him, and fell with him, in his first transgression"; that is, the covenant having been made for Adam's posterity his guilt was imputed to them. The catechism continues, "The sinfulness of that estate whereunto men fell, consists in, the guilt of Adam's first sin, the want of original righteousness, and the corruption of his whole nature, which is commonly called original sin." Some one may feel that this was unjust. I have been told that it is utterly foreign to even imagine that God could punish men, today, for what Adam did so long ago. If that be true, then it is impossible also for us to be saved by what Christ did so long ago. At the heart of the Bible teaching is the doctrine of imputation. The guilt of Adam was imputed to us. The righteousness of Christ may be imputed to those who are saved. And the sins of those who are saved are imputed to Christ, for which He suffered on the cross.

There is ample evidence of the Fall and the resultant wickedness of the human heart in the world. Jesus addressed the Pharisees with the following words: "Either make the tree good, and its fruit good; or else make the tree corrupt, and its fruit corrupt; for the tree is known by his fruit. O generation of vipers, how can ye, being evil, speak good things? For out of the abundance of the heart the mouth speaketh. A good man out of the good treasure of the heart bringeth forth good things: and an evil man out of the evil treasure bringeth forth evil things." Later He said, "Those things which proceed out of the mouth come forth from the heart and they defile a man. For out of the heart proceed evil thoughts, murders, adulteries, fornications, thefts, false

The Wicked Heart

witness, blasphemies: these are the things which defile a man." The Scriptures describe the seat of man's fallen nature as the flesh. That does not mean the physical flesh. It is the fleshly principle or the wicked heart. The fruits of the flesh are listed as "adultery, fornication, uncleanness, lasciviousness . . . wrath, hatred, strife" and other similar evils which if men do, they cannot inherit the kingdom of God. The history of civilization, whether taken from secular books or from Paul's account in the first chapter of Romans, shows that mankind is fallen, depraved, guilty and wicked.

II. THIS WICKEDNESS OF THE HEART IS THE UNIVERSAL CONDITION OF MAN.

Wickedness is universal—that is, it is not limited to any class of men or to any particular sins of men. A professor under whom I once studied claimed that the conception of the wickedness of man was not Biblical. "It might be Pauline," he said, "but it isn't the conception either of the Old Testament or of Jesus." We need only turn to the Bible to see what it has to say about men. It is granted that Paul includes all under sin. A portion of the first chapter of Romans is given over to a description of the downward progress of man from the beginning until the condition of heathenism with its idolatry and repulsive forms of sin that existed. The second chapter is devoted to establishing the inexcusableness of man, whether a Jew who had the law written externally or a Gentile who possessed the law written upon his heart. The third chapter reveals Jew and Gentile alike having broken the law. The summary is given in these words, "We have before proved both Jews and Gentiles, that they are all under sin, as it is written, there is none righteous no not one: there is none that understandeth, there is none that seeketh after God. They are all gone out of the way. They are altogether become unprofitable. There is none that doeth good, no not one." Paul claims that the law stops every mouth from professing righteousness, that all the world may become guilty before God.

We turn back to the message of John the Baptist and we find that he called all men to repentance because of their sin. He made no exceptions—not even the Pharisees, whom he called a generation of vipers, nor the common people nor himself. For when Jesus came he said to him, "I have need to be baptized of thee and comest thou to me?" John the Baptist believed men were sinners. Now when Jesus began to preach did He change this message? Did He repudiate the accusation of John? Not at all. He preached, "Repent, for the kingdom of heaven is at hand." Moreover, He said that John the Baptist was not only a prophet but the greatest man who had been born of woman. Let us remember that Jesus in speaking to His disciples said that they were evil; that it was Jesus who proclaimed the Parable of the Pharisee and the Publican, the one being condemned in his self-righteousness and the other being justified out of his confession of sin. It was also Jesus who told the rich young ruler who believed that he kept all the commandments that he lacked one thing, that is, poverty of spirit. No proud or self-righteous man can enter the kingdom of God.

The Wicked Heart

The wickedness of the heart is total and not partial. The Catechism says, "All mankind, by their fall, lost communion with God, are under His wrath and curse and so made liable to all the miseries of this life, to death itself, and to the pains of hell forever." We speak of total depravity, total inability to save ourselves, total helplessness in the face of sin. This is a correct description of the condition of man. Against it there are those who followed Pelagius, the British monk of centuries ago, who believed that each man was perfectly able to follow his own choice, that he was the captain of his soul and the master of his fate. He believed that the Fall had no effect on us whatsoever. Some of our religious people of today are followers of Pelagius. In some churches where the Apostles' Creed has been discarded another creed has been substituted which begins, "I believe in man." These moderns believe in man's goodness, in man's ability to save himself, in man's self-sufficiency. The Bible knows nothing of such a view. Moreover, the limited experience of this speaker in human affairs gives no support to such a view. There are others who go half way with Pelagius. They say man is sick, he is weak, he cannot save himself but he can co-operate with God or he can merely not resist the Spirit and God's Word, but when we analyze this it resolves itself into the question, "Who saves an individual? Is it God or man?" Even if only co-operation or non-resistance are involved the answer must be man, but the Bible answer is God. He only is able to save from the uttermost to the uttermost.

The only exception to this condition of universal

wickedness of heart is the Lord Jesus Christ. He was the second Adam. He perfectly obeyed the covenant of works or of life. He was born of the Holy Ghost and of Mary. He was the "lamb without spot or blemish." It was altogether fitting that He should be the Saviour and in the Infinite wisdom of God the sin of Adam and the sins of the believers of all ages were imputed unto Him, so that by the steps of His humiliation, including birth and dedication in the temple, the baptism of John, suffering in Gethsemane, and finally the death on the cross when He became sin for us, He took our guilt away.

III. THIS WICKEDNESS LEAVES NO HELP FOR MAN EXCEPT IN CHRIST.

Like as Peter replied when Jesus asked the disciples if they too should go away, we would declare our helplessness with the words, "Lord to whom shall we go? Thou hast the words of eternal life and we believe and are sure that Thou art the Christ, the Son of the living God." Those of us that are honest with ourselves admit that we bear the image of the First Adam. We know that the menace of death is ahead. We know that we are subject to the miseries of this life. We are certain that there is to be a place of punishment after death. We are too well aware of the barrier that stands between us and God designating our lost communion, and we confess our want of righteousness and our corruption of nature or of heart which is the cause of our transgression. Now if we bear the image of the earthly why should we not also bear the image of the heavenly?

The Wicked Heart

Paul said, "The first man Adam was made a living soul: the last Adam was made a quickening spirit. Howbeit that was not first which is spiritual but that which is natural, and afterward that which is spiritual. The first man is of the earth, earthy, the second man is the Lord from heaven. As is the earthy such are they also that are earthy: and as is the heavenly such are they also that are heavenly. And as we have borne the image of the earthy we shall also bear the image of the heavenly. Now this I say, brethren, that flesh and blood cannot inherit the kingdom of God."

Surely that is plain. That means that by the works of righteousness a man can not change his nature. It is impossible for an evil nature to do good. He may have a veneer of morality and kindness and he may receive less punishment than one who is overtly wicked, but he has no righteousness in the eyes of God, for by the works of the law there shall no flesh be justified in His sight. There is no difference for all have sinned and come short of the glory of God. Let no man, then, trust in the arm of the flesh, for it will fail him.

Though there is no help for man in himself or in any human moral code, there is a balm of Gilead which is effectual in the healing of the soul. The heart of man, that is his nature, must and may be re-made, re-created and transformed. Jesus spoke to a good man as far as human nature goes when He talked to Nicodemus but He said to him, "Except a man be born again, he cannot see the kingdom of God. . . . except a man be born of water and the spirit he can not enter

into the kingdom of God. That which is born of the
flesh is flesh; and that which is born of the spirit is
spirit: marvel not that I said unto thee ye must be born
again." That new birth may take place, as Peter said,
by cleansing with the precious blood of Jesus and by
obedience to the truth. This is being born again not
of corruptible seed but of incorruptible, by the word
of God which liveth and abideth for ever. John adds,
"He that believeth that Jesus is the Christ is born of
God." This regeneration of man's heart, this change
of his nature from wickedness to goodness changes the
source of all of his actions, of all of his affections and
of all of his thoughts; by purging the source he has
purged the stream and life itself is transformed.

When Solomon became king he administered justice
on those who had done evil during the latter days of
David's reign. Among others, he called unto him
Shimei, who had cursed David and who had performed
much evil. He commanded that he should not leave
Jerusalem for good or for evil, saying "on the day
that thou goest out, and passest over the brook Kidron,
thou shalt know for certain that thou shalt surely die."
Shimei answered, "The saying is good: as my lord the
king hath said, so will thy servant do." He dwelt at
Jerusalem for three years. Then he pursued two servants to Gath. When he returned King Solomon sent
for him. He came to the court. Solomon recalled the
condition on which he had permitted Shimei to live
and then added, "Thou knowest all the wickedness
which thine heart is privy to, that thou didst to David
my father: therefore the Lord shall return thy wicked-

The Wicked Heart

ness upon thine own head." He then commanded that Shimei be executed.

God is a great judge. His judgments will be according to righteousness. He is the knower of the human heart, therefore, the wise course for us who know all the wickedness that our hearts are privy to is to accept the Divine command to repent, to turn unto the means of heart-cleansing and to obey His Word. Had Shimei obeyed Solomon's limiting command which he first placed upon him, he would not have been executed. Those who obey the Divine call to repentance will never face the Lord in His vengeance on a wicked heart. Let us honestly confess our condition and seek the Divine grace. Then Christian affections and Christian life will rise, as a pure stream from an artesian well, deep in a pure heart.

"Upon the cross of Jesus mine eye at times can see
The very dying form of One who suffered there for me;
And from my smitten heart with tears two wonders
    I confess,
The wonders of His glorious love, and my own worthlessness.

"I take, O cross, thy shadow for my abiding place:
I ask no other sunshine than the sunshine of His face;
Content to let the world go by, to know no gain or loss;
My sinful self my only shame, my glory all the cross."

III.

THE PRICKED HEART

"Now when they heard this, they were pricked in their heart, and said unto Peter and to the rest of the apostles, Men and brethren, what shall we do?"
—ACTS 2:37.

THE phrase, "A Pricked Heart" is nothing other than a synonym for conviction of sin—a belief not very largely held in the religious world, today. Moreover, the condition described by this term is almost unknown. It is obvious that if we reject the idea of sin as a concept acceptable to the modern mind, we cannot make any room for such an experience as conviction. The state of sinfulness and the various sins which arise out of it, are definite transgressions of the majestic law of God. It is the law which brings to us the sense of sin.

Psychologists in their own language reinforce this fact of conviction of sin. They ascribe it to conflict between standards of achievement worthy of ourselves and the frustration of falling short of them, to resultant neuroses, to lack of balance between periods of tranquility and excitement, to tension, to the prevalence of "unpleasurable" states of mind and to psychological maladjustment. For the most part physchologists substitute these explanations for any religious emphasis. Some of them might even ridicule that. They might suggest that there was a repressed experience needing the relief brought through the hands of a psychoanalyst. But a study of the experience of the saints through the ages will definitely convince us of the fact of conviction for sin and the need of removal of this through Christ.

In describing his experience, Cowper said: "One moment I thought myself shut out from mercy by one chapter, and the next by another. The sword of the Spirit seemed to guard the tree of life from my touch and to flame against me in every avenue by which I attempted to approach it. I particularly remember that the parable of the barren fig tree was to me an inconceivable source of anguish; and I applied it to myself, with a strong persuasion in my mind that when our Saviour pronounced a curse upon it He had me in His eye and pointed that curse directly at me." Cowper felt himself exceedingly sinful.

D'Aubigne, the famous author of *The History of the Reformation,* describes his experience of conviction. He had been attending the University of Geneva where the professor of Divinity had confined himself to lecturing on Immortality of the Soul and the Existence of God. He did not believe in the Trinity and instead of quoting from the Bible, he used Seneca and Plato whom he held up to the admiration of the students. "But the Lord sent one of His servants to Geneva," says D'Aubigne, "and I well remember the visit of Robert Haldane. I heard of him first as an English or Scotch gentleman who spoke much about the Bible, which seemed a very strange thing to me and the other students to whom it was a closed book. I afterwards met Mr. Haldane at a private house, along with some other friends, and heard him read from the English Bible a chapter from Romans about the natural corruption of man—a doctrine of which I had never heard. In fact I was quite astonished to hear of men being corrupt by nature. I remember saying to Mr. Haldane, 'Now I see that doctrine in the Bible.' 'Yes,' he replied, 'but do you see it in your heart?' That was a simple question; but it came home to my conscience. It was the sword of the Spirit and from that time I saw that my heart was corrupt and I knew from the Word of God that I could be saved by grace alone."

These are but two of many possible illustrations we might draw. Augustine experienced intense pricking of the heart in the garden at Milan before a text from Romans brought healing to his soul. Luther endured heart agony through the long days at the Black cloister of the Augustinian monastery at Erfurt, until Scripture verses quoted by John von Staupitz brought him healing. John Wesley entered his period of conviction during a storm at sea on a voyage to America, when he saw the calmness of the Moravians in the face of death. Not till some years later at Aldersgate Chapel was his burden of conviction lifted. He had gone to the American colonies to convert the Indians, and he returned to England needing someone to convert him. Peter Bohler's sermon from Romans brought healing in the form of a "strange warming of my heart."

The Pricked Heart 43

The loss of experience of conviction is due to the failure on the part of the Church to honor the Holy Spirit whose specific work this is. Jesus said to His disciples, "It is expedient for you that I go away: for if I go not away, the Comforter will not come unto you; but if I depart, I will send Him unto you. And when he is come, he will reprove the world of sin, and of righteousness, and of judgment." Only the Holy Spirit can produce conviction in the heart. No human teacher can do it. The law or the Gospel in any of its forms cannot do it; even the Word of God is unable to perform this task. Only when the Holy Spirit attends these other instruments with His Presence and His discerning power does conviction result. In fact, Jesus would have become a man — would have died on the cross—in vain, and mankind could not have been saved, without this conviction of the Holy Spirit. It is the Spirit who discovers the sin in the heart. One has said, "You see not the motes in the air, though numerous as the leaved forest, till the glowing ray of sunlight reveals them to the eye. The river seems to flow stainless and clear till the wondrous microscope displays to the view myriads of loathsome creatures inclosed in every drop that glitters beneath the sun." Thus it is also that we only recognize the wickedness of our hearts when the Holy Spirit illumines them with the light of His Presence. If a man will take a Greek concordance of the New Testament and see how often the words *pneuma* and *pneuma hagion* are used by sacred writers, he will learn how prominent a part the Holy Spirit takes in saving men and how hopeless is the case of men who are left to themselves. The Holy Spirit is the agent that produces the conviction and the change of heart of an individual. He also effectually accomplishes regeneration and He is the source of spiritual life and all of its exercises.

Herein we understand the deadly effect of Modernism and of Unitarianism. Both systems profess to believe in God but deny the personality of the Holy Spirit. These two perversions of Christian truth are unable to produce the least semblance even of Christian experience and affections, for the entire source of these is cut off. The profession of adherence to either of these heresies is worse than praying that God would remove His Holy Spirit from us, for the latter although sinning grievously, is still based upon the belief in the existence of the Holy Spirit. The atrophied condition of the Church is due, largely, to the fact that Modernists and Unitarians are able to tell moving stories which affect the emotions or the intellect without God touching the heart or the depth of man's personality.

This has resulted in multitudes of people being received into the Church without ever having been convicted of sin, or realizing the insufficiency of their own efforts, or of being regenerated by the power of God. To such individuals, the Bible is a closed book. A Canadian preacher only this summer told of visiting in a church where a celebration was being held to mark the receiving of three hundred members into the church. It had been a successful calling campaign. The leading woman in the campaign had been a member of the church for only one year. The argument used to bring her in was based upon the value of the church to her large real estate holdings in the community. She, in turn, had used the same argument and had effectively enrolled scores in the community church. That kind of practice is altogether too general and cannot but result in the degradation of the Church. Contrast it, if you will, with New Testament methods of bringing new members into the infant Church.

I. THE TRUTH WHICH PRICKS THE HEART; OR CONVICTION PRODUCED.

Our text says, "When they heard this, they were pricked in their heart." What is it that Peter told the multitude on the day of Pentecost which caused the people to be smitten in heart and to realize their need of being saved? While Peter preached about a number of doctrines there are three which stand out as the emphasized facts of this great sermon. It would be very rewarding, sometime, to analyze this sermon of Peter as an example of true doctrinal preaching.

The first of the three emphasized points was that of the wickedness of man. How did Peter make this plain? He said: "Ye men of Israel hear these words; Jesus of Nazareth, a man approved of God among you by miracles and wonders and signs, which God did by him in the midst of you, as ye yourselves also know: him, being delivered by the determinate counsel and foreknowledge of God, ye have taken, and by wicked hands have crucified and slain." What was in the heart of man that would cause him to slay such an one as Jesus? Here is the greatest example of native wickedness of which we have any record. If it is true that a good life, one spent in helping others, in kindliness and in noble teaching, wins the admiration and support of mankind, how can we explain the historical fact of these Jews and Gentiles putting Jesus to death? No one could convict Him of sin. No one could recall a single evil deed which He ever performed; yet they wanted to put Him out of the way. The reason, of course, was that the beauty, holiness and nobility of the life of Jesus revealed the wickedness of their lives, and they wanted to put Him out of the way. What greater proof could we desire of the depravity of man? To be sure, the Bible joins this statement of man's wickedness in crucifying Jesus with a declaration that it was done "by the determinate counsel of God." The Bible teaches that the death of Christ was absolutely necessary; that if there had been any other way in which man could be saved, Christ is dead in vain. If men are an unfallen, uncorrupted race, and if they can be preserved from sin by a mere change of their circumstances, why should there have been the costly array of remedial means, the incarnation, the sufferings and death of the eternal Son of God for their salvation? Obviously, the first truth which pricked the hearts of the people was the doctrine of depravity.

The second truth which Peter emphasized and which produced conviction among this multitude was that of the goodness of God. He said: "This Jesus hath God raised up, whereof we are all witnesses; therefore being by the right hand of God exalted, and having re-

The Pricked Heart   47

ceived of the Father the promise of the Holy Ghost, he hath shed forth this, which ye now see and hear." God's plan had been rejected by the people. They had spurned their Messiah, declaring that they had no king but Cæsar, and yet God now sent to them the Holy Spirit and gave them another chance. Have you ever thought of the goodness of God? Remember how God dealt with men during what is called the dispensation of the Father. He made covenants with them, He sent the prophets, He entrusted them with revelations and He performed miracles on their behalf, but for the most part their hearts were hardened and they rejected these many graces. Though some were cut off because of their sin, God in His goodness still gave them another chance. In the fulness of time He sent His only begotten Son to be born of a woman, to live under the law and to be obedient unto death that they might believe upon Him, that they might love Him and follow Him. And what did they do? They persecuted Him, rejected Him and crucified Him. Now Peter stood forth and said that God had fulfilled the promises of Christ and had shed forth the Holy Ghost, the third Person of the Trinity, and that He was a gift to be made to all those who would repent of their sins and believe upon the Lord Jesus Christ. This Holy Spirit is the Comforter, the Paraclete, the One who empowers the believer, whom God in His goodness, not being willing that any should perish, sent into the world to continue the work of redemption. This goodness of God revealed their own wickedness all along and convicted them. Paul says that the goodness of God leadeth men to repentance, but that the despising of this goodness treasures up wrath on the impenitent heart against the day of revelation of the righteous judgment of God.

The third truth which Peter emphasized was that of a future judgment at the hands of the Jesus whom they had rejected and crucified. "Whom God hath raised up," he cried, "having loosed the pains of death: because it was not possible that He should be holden of it. For David speaketh concerning Him, I foresaw the Lord always before my face for He is on my right hand, that I should not be moved: Therefore did my heart rejoice, and my tongue was glad; moreover also my flesh shall rest in hope: because Thou wilt not leave my soul in hell, neither wilt thou suffer thine holy One to see corruption . . . David . . . seeing this before, spake of the resurrection of Christ, that His soul was not left in hell, neither did his flesh see corruption . . . for David is not ascended into the heavens; but he saith himself, the Lord saith unto my Lord, sit Thou on My right hand, until I make Thy foes Thy footstool. Therefore let all the house of Israel know assuredly, that God hath made that same Jesus, whom ye have crucified, both Lord and Christ." Peter had infallible proofs that Jesus had risen from the dead. He had seen Him ascend into heaven and he had the promise that Jesus was coming again to judge the quick and the dead. Jesus is the Man set for the judgment of the world. He said to His disciples, "Many will say to Me in that day, Lord, Lord, . . . have we not in thy Name done many wonderful works?"

Peter knew that the prophets and Jesus Himself

had foretold this judgment. It was the thought in the minds of these Israelites that the same Jesus whom they rejected and crucified would determine their destinies through eternity that convicted them. We have need of this iron in our preaching today. There is all too little of the proclamation of judgment, of hell and of punishment. The story is told concerning the original portrait of Bishop Asbury which was made in Baltimore. It once hung over the fireplace of a planter's parlor in Maryland where a bed had been made for one of his men, beastly drunk. Here he was laid down entirely insensible. Just as the day was breaking, and the rays of light were dimly fallen upon the portrait, he began to awake from his drunken stupor. His eyes fell upon the uplifted hand of the venerable bishop and he fearfully fancied the judgment had come and that the divine King with upraised arm was about to pronounce the last sentence of condemnation upon him. The sight and thought produced a powerful impression upon his mind leading him to repentance, amendment, and conversion. Our wickedness, God's goodness, the judgment, these are the truths among others which produce conviction.

II. THE EXPERIENCE OF A PRICKED HEART OR CONVICTION.

The text says, "they were pricked in their heart." This is not an unusual experience. The patriarch Job is represented in the Bible as the best man of his generation, but even he placed his hand upon his mouth and prostrated himself in the dust before God, declaring that he abhorred himself, that he was vile, and repented in dust and ashes. Isaiah cried out, "Woe is me! . . . I am a man of unclean lips and I dwell in the midst of a people of unclean lips." Even Spurgeon, for fifty years one of the greatest of English preachers, said, "I have known what it is to tread the earth and fear lest every tuft of grass should but cover a door to hell; trembling lest every particle, and every atom, and every stone should be so at league with God against me as to destroy me." This describes the state of conviction. It is a miserable poignant feeling of self-aversion and impotence. It may best be described by the words of the suffering Job: "I have said to corruption, thou art my father; to the worm, thou art my mother."

Paul, before he was converted, was under conviction. Jesus said to him on the road to Damascus, "It is hard for thee to kick against the pricks." We are not to think that Paul—Saul as he was then named—had been ready to believe upon Jesus and only needed a hallucination on the Damascus road to lead him to believe. But we may be assured that he knew a great deal about Jesus by extorting confessions from the Christians whom he persecuted and wished to see put to death. He had learned all the necessary facts of the Gospel concerning Jesus' miracles, His sinless life, His crucifixion, His resurrection and His teaching, but he did not believe these things. Before he could believe them it was necessary for Christ to appear to him, yet his condition is described by Jesus as kicking against the pricks, as a horse kicks against the goad.

The Pricked Heart   51

God had given him knowledge and experience to bring him under conviction and Paul had sought escape from his miserable self by persecuting the believing Jews. He sought relief from his frustration by activity in the form of pleasing a misunderstood Deity.

David's experience was not altogether different. He had been guilty of a very cruel sin, one about which we shall have more to say in the next talk. It had wounded the woman very deeply. It had cost the life of one of his best friends and separated him from God and it had brought him to such self-aversion that he described his condition by saying, "My sin is ever before me." Yet David delayed in his repentance of this sin. Ever under conviction, he tried to find relief in war and we read that David was guilty of great cruelty to the enemies of Israel whom he conquered. He tormented them physically, as the degenerated nations were wont to torture their captives. This was utterly unlike David and we can only lay it to his miserable condition of heart and life during the time of conviction for his sin and before he repented and was forgiven. The tenderness of his heart which caused him to be smitten with conviction when he but cut off the skirt of Saul's garment in the wilderness, because he was the anointed of the Lord, at this time smote him to the full. Pity the soul which is under conviction!

Contrast this condition with the uncondemned heart. John said: "Beloved, if our heart condemn us not, then have we confidence toward God." This confidence arises out of a sense of peace, of pardon, of personal fellowship, and of keeping His commandments. It results in the religious affections of joy, love, and thankfulness. During conviction the religious affections reach their lowest point. When the heart is pure and uncondemned they rise to their fulness.

III. THE HEALING OF A PRICKED HEART, OR CONVERSION.

The people to whom Peter preached, when pricked in heart, cried, "What shall we do?" Whenever a man is convicted he is also overcome with a sense of personal inability to lift himself out of this condition. Paul deals with the situation fully in the seventh chapter of Romans. He tells of two laws which are warring in his members, that of sin and that of desiring to do good. Finally he cried in helplessness, "O wretched man that I am! who shall deliver me from the body of this death?" This is an expression of inability. Of course that inability, as we mentioned in the last sermon, deals only with the things of the Spirit. Man is capable of natural and of moral good but not of spiritual. We discussed this fully in the last sermon. Man is totally unable to save himself.

If the pricked and suffering heart is thus to be healed it must be done by the great Physician. Jesus said, "Come unto Me, all ye that labour and are heavy laden, and I will give you rest. Take My yoke upon you, and learn of Me; for I am meek and lowly in heart: and ye shall find rest unto your souls." Jesus' lowly heart is touched with our burden of sin. Remember that Jesus said, "I am not come to call the righteous, but sinners to repentance." It is only when we take our stand with the publican, with the returning prodigal and with the helpless leper that we can receive the ministration of the Physician, but when He turns His power to the diseases of the soul, He is able to heal. We should remember, however, that conviction is not conversion. Felix illustrates this truth. Paul stood before him and reasoned concerning righteousness, temperance, and judgment to come. Felix trembled under conviction and answered, "Go thy way for this time; when I have a convenient season, I will call for thee." Felix's conviction left him and we have no record of his ever being saved.

Peter told the men of Israel what they should do when they experienced this conviction. He said, "Repent, and be baptized every one of you in the Name of Jesus for the remission of sins, and ye shall receive the gift of the Holy Ghost. For the promise is unto you, and to your children, and to all that are afar off, even as many as the Lord our God shall call." If you are under conviction, if God blesses you by troubling you over your sins, He has extended to you the promise of salvation. Follow your conviction with a godly sorrow, with a true turning away from your sin, and with an active faith and trust in the Lord Jesus Christ. This is your part. The gift of the Holy Ghost is God's part. The Holy Spirit, who has been with you pointing out your sins and restraining you from wickedness, will now take up His abode in your heart, thereby regenerating, re-creating you and bringing His attendant gifts such as faith, love, joy and peace. This is the promise.

The result of this sermon and of this conviction of

heart was that great numbers gladly received Peter's word and were baptized. Well may a minister be thankful when the people receive this message with gladness and with evidence of conversion, but we are not unaware that the same message producing conviction sometimes results in opposition. When Peter testified before the Sanhedrin concerning Jesus, "they were cut to the heart when they heard his word and took counsel to slay him." Their conviction resulted in further evil. Likewise when Stephen stood before that council and testified concerning what God had done, "they were cut to the heart," and being so full of anger they led Stephen out and stoned him to death. The preaching of the truth of God must result in one of these two attitudes, either true conversion or opposition, and many a faithful witness has been the victim of convicted but unbelieving hearts.

IV.

THE CONTRITE HEART

"The sacrifices of God are a broken spirit: a broken and a contrite heart, O God, Thou wilt not despise."
—Ps. 51:17.

"The Lord is nigh unto them that are of a broken heart; and saveth such as be of a contrite spirit."
—Ps. 34:18.

THE sermon on "The Pricked Heart" ended with the command to repent. "Repent . . . and ye shall receive the gift of the Holy Ghost," said Peter. Repentance is a word repeated so often in the history of the Church as to be emptied of its meaning. Yet it was not so in the beginning.

When John the Baptist came preaching repentance he stirred the latent consciences of the multitude and brought them to their knees before God. To them, the word "repentance" meant definite action. They asked him, "What shall we do, then?" To the rich, John said, "He that hath two coats, let him impart to him that hath none; and he that hath meat, let him do likewise." To the publicans he said, "Exact no more than that which is appointed you." To the soldiers, he said, "Do violence to no man, neither accuse any falsely; and be content with your wages." To the multitude

John said, "Bring forth fruits worthy of repentance." The people were impressed by him. When Jesus came preaching repentance, a similar stir was made. We read that great multitudes followed Him out of the cities unto a mountain "and when He was set, His disciples came unto Him: and He taught them, saying, Blessed are the poor in spirit: for theirs is the kingdom of heaven." What followed was the Sermon on the Mount.

Paul is described as testifying both to the Jews and to the Greeks, "repentance toward God, and faith toward our Lord Jesus Christ." Thus also it was with Peter on the day of Pentecost, when such a profound change occurred in the life of thousands of Jews. Repentance has been preached through the centuries by the great ministers of God, but there were times when the message fell upon deaf ears. Such a time the present seems to be. The preacher of repentance today is widely looked upon as standing upon the periphery of Christian service. The modern day places social reform at the heart of Christian activity and thought, but the day will come sooner or later when the word "repent" will once again fall upon pricked hearts and when it does it will be well if we know the meaning of the word.

The kind of repentance of which Peter spoke is the same as that declared by the giants of preaching which results in amendment of life and regeneration of nature. Repentance must go deeper than the surface eddies of the stream of life. This kind of repentance consists of three steps—conviction, contrition and conver-

The Contrite Heart

sion. Conviction has already been dealt with in a former chapter. Conviction is the work of the Holy Spirit applying the changeless truths of God's revelation to the heart of man. It is the experience of inner condemnation and self-aversion entered upon by the sinner and it should lead one to the Gospel as the means of his healing. Contrition goes one step beyond conviction. A man may be convicted of his sin and still not turn unto Christ. Such was the case of Felix and of Agrippa and of the rich young ruler. The next step following conviction is contrition. This consists of sorrow of heart toward God for sin. But even contrition is not sufficient for salvation, as we shall see, for this is still subjective. It must result in conversion or the amendment of character and habits.

Historically, contrition, or penitence, has been confused with penance. This is the great age-long error of the Roman Catholic Church. Basically, the Roman Church is sound on the subject of contrition. The Council of Trent defined contrition as follows: " . . . Contrition, which holds the first place in the above mentioned acts of the penitent (that is, contrition, confession and satisfaction) is the sorrow and detestation which the mind feels to a past sin, with a purpose of sinning no more. Now this emotion of contrition was always necessary in order to obtain the pardon of sin; and when a man has sinned after baptism, it prepares him for the remission of sin, if joined with confidence in the mercy of God, and an earnest desire of performing whatever is necessary to the proper reception of the sacrament (that is, penance)." This sorrow of heart or *contritio cordis* is Biblical, but the Roman Church goes on to spoil its statement by making it possible for those who do not manifest true contrition to be saved by substitutionary means. The Canons of Trent say: "Imperfect contrition, which is called attrition, commonly arising from a consideration of the turpitude of sin and a fear of hell and punishment, the intention of continuing in sin with the hope of receiving pardon at last being disavowed, not only does not make a man a hypocrite and a greater sinner, but is really a gift of God and an impulse of the Holy Spirit: not that the Spirit does as yet dwell in the soul, but merely excites the penitent, who, thus aided, prepares his way to righteousness. And although it cannot of itself conduct the sinner to justification without the sacrament of penance, yet it disposes him to seek the grace of God in the sacrifice of penance." Now if attrition with penance and priestly absolution are sufficient before God for justification, then imperfect repentance is all that is necessary for the salvation of the sinner.

This doctrine of penance has externalized the Christian religion, whereas it should be a matter of the heart. It is still practiced by the Roman Catholics, although it probably reached its most blatant form in the time of Martin Luther when representatives of the Pope were empowered to sell the forgiveness of sin before it was committed. John Tetzel, who preached near to Luther's parish, crassly told the people that by the time the coin hit the bottom of the indulgence box their sins were forgiven. Luther immediately recognized the

The Contrite Heart

effect of this in the confessional by the lack of contrition of heart and it resulted in his ninety-five theses, nailed to the door of the Schloss-kirche in Wittenberg. Repentance can never remain merely a matter of externals. It must contain a true sorrow of heart for the sins committed.

The emphasis of this sermon is laid on the godly sorrow of the heart. Both texts of the sermon are taken from the Psalmist David, and well may David speak with authority concerning this matter of contrition for sin. We said above that contrition results from conviction of one's sin. The second book of Samuel tells fully the story of David's sin. First he was tempted, in a careless moment. Then he played with the vision of pleasurable indulgence. Then he pushed from his mind the Divine law, his human obligations, and personal integrity, all of which would be violated by his sin. Like the woman in the garden of Eden, David decided to know evil by experiencing it, and he fell into heinous sin. The king of Israel had been a man after God's own heart; he had been the anointed of the Lord. Now he became guilty of conscience, pricked in heart, miserable in mind, and full of hatred of himself. It was a true experience of conviction. Out of this condition David was able to write the Fifty-first Psalm, which was the outward manifestation of his sorrow of heart before God, because of his sin.

We have said that sorrow of heart should result in conversion of life. These external manifestations of true repentance must be left for the subject of faith or "The Believing Heart," for faith carries with it another meaning besides trust, and that is faithfulness. Such a subject might well be called "Conversion." Hence, in our future discussion, we hope to correct this misunderstanding concerning the nature of faith which results in its being treated subjectively alone.

About this sorrow of heart we would observe, first, this sorrow of heart may be according to the world; second, this sorrow of heart may be according to God; third, this godly sorrow of heart should result in conversion.

I. Sorrow of Heart May Be According to the World.

To the Christians at Corinth Paul wrote: "I rejoice, not that ye were made sorry, but that ye sorrowed to repentance: for ye were made sorry after a godly manner . . . for godly sorrow worketh repentance to salvation not to be repented of: but the sorrow of the world worketh death." There is a sorrow "according to God" and there is a sorrow "according to the world" over one's sin. The latter has often been called remorse or attrition. It is imperfect contrition.

The nature of this attrition is quite distinct from the nature of contrition. The name itself was first introduced by the schoolmen in the twelfth century to distinguish between perfect and imperfect repentance. The result was the formulation of the doctrine of penance, which then became a sacrament. The elevation of works to a place in the means of salvation by the Roman Church arrogated to the priesthood a greater sacerdotal power—that of remitting or retaining the sins of individuals. Christ never gave such power to the Church and there is no reason to believe that attrition will ever result in salvation. It consists in sorrow for the consequences of sin, sorrow because of its discovery before men, sorrow because of social or Divine punishment. Attrition reveals a weak, cowardly soul which is afraid of the consequences of action in this world or the world to come, but will not abandon the actions themselves. Such might be described in the following words: "Who knowing the judgment of God, that they which commit such things are worthy of death, not only do the same, but have pleasure in them that do them." Those experiencing attrition or remorse have no thought of the heinousness of the act of sin itself. They are controlled only by a kind of self-pity that they were found out. The nature of attrition may best be described as negative, retrospective, and emotional. The New Testament uses an entirely different word for this experience from what it uses for contrition. Attrition is *metamelomai*. Contrition is *metanoia*. They are entirely different.

The nature of this attrition may best be understood by glancing at some of the characters who manifested it. Saul, the first king of Israel, was given a full opportunity to obey the Lord and to establish his house. He persistently disobeyed the commands of God, however, by arrogating to himself the priestly function, by refusing to destroy the Amalekites and by seeking the death of David. When Saul first sinned he said, "I forced myself" because of the people. There was no repentance in that. It was self-justification. When he next sinned and was told by Samuel that the Lord had rent the kingdom from him he cried, "I have sinned: yet honor me now, I pray thee, before the elders of my people and before Israel, and turn again with me, that I may worship the Lord thy God." Saul showed no contrition for his sin. He was merely sorry that God's great prophet had broken from him and that the people would be divided in their allegiance between the two. His only sorrow was that sufficient to reconcile himself to Samuel publicly. Three times in Saul's life he said, "I have sinned," but we have no record of Saul ever manifesting a true repentance.

In the days of Elijah, Ahab was king of Israel, whose wife was the wicked Jezebel. They had just finished with the murder of Naboth and the seizure of his vineyard. The word of the Lord came unto Elijah saying, "Thus shalt thou speak unto Ahab . . . In the place where dogs licked the blood of Naboth shall dogs lick thy blood, even thine." It came to pass that when Ahab heard those words "he rent his clothes, and put on sackcloth upon his flesh, and fasted, and lay in sackcloth, and went softly." Ahab repented outwardly, but the very next chapter tells how he continued in his wicked life. There was no true contrition for sin.

A splendid young man, unexcelled in natural gifts and in worldly position, came to Jesus seeking the way to eternal life. He was self-righteous and confident that he obeyed the law fully. He was proud in spirit. Jesus said to him, "If thou wilt be perfect, go and sell that thou hast, and give to the poor, and thou shalt have treasure in heaven: and come and follow me." Jesus was telling the young man that he must be poor in

The Contrite Heart 63

spirit if he was to find eternal life. The young man had recognized the fact that he did not possess eternal life, but when he heard this saying, "he went away sorrowful: for he had great possessions." His sorrow was not according to God for his sin. His sorrow was according to the world. He never followed Jesus.

One of the twelve disciples manifested this kind of attrition. He had been chosen by Jesus to have a part in the apostleship, but he had taken his eyes off Christ and turned them to the world. He looked upon conditions rather than on the Conqueror of those conditions and gradually he was led into the despicable act of selling Jesus for thirty pieces of silver. After the crucifixion was over we read, "Then Judas, which had betrayed Him, when he saw that He was condemned, repented himself, and brought again the thirty pieces of silver to the chief priests and elders, saying, I have sinned in that I have betrayed innocent blood." He cast down the pieces of silver and departed and went out and hanged himself. Judas repented. Judas was sorrowful, but his sorrow was not that which led him to faith. It rather confirmed him in his wickedness. It was remorse because of the consequences of his deed.

The practice of affecting or pretending contrition is old. The Jews inflicted austerities and penalties upon themselves by fasting, by wearing sackcloth and ashes, by praying publicly in a repentant attitude. Even, today, one may stop at any time by the ancient wall of the Herodian temple and see Jews wailing out their penitence. It has an aspect of externalism to it. It is very similar to Romish penance. There, if the contrition is intense, the temporal punishment is remitted. If it is not intense, pilgrimages, gifts, candles, prayers and other good works are made to complement it. Among the English Puritans of the seventeenth century, and particularly in the Church of Scotland, it was a common thing to make satisfaction publicly on the stool of repentance. The laws were impartially executed for peers and commoners alike. It is healthy that today in the Church penitential humiliations are no longer in favor. We are closer to Jesus' attitude. To His disciples He said: "When thou prayest, thou shalt not be as the hypocrites are: for they love to pray standing in the synagogues and in the corners of the streets, that they may be seen of men . . . but thou, when thou prayest enter into thy closet, and when thou hast shut thy door, pray to thy Father which is in secret; and thy Father which seeth in secret shall reward thee openly . . .when ye fast, be not, as the hypocrites, of a sad countenance: for they disfigure their faces, that they may appear unto men to fast . . . but thou, when thou fastest, anoint thy head, and wash thy face; that thou appear not unto men to fast . . . for God looketh upon the heart."

II. SORROW OF HEART—ATTRITION ACCORDING TO GOD.

Sorrow of the godly sort is contrition or real repentance. This is different from attrition. Here is a desire for deliverance from sin rather than a sense of danger of wrath or exposure. Contrition has its source in saving faith rather than unbelief. Contrition comes from love to God and to His laws rather than an aversion to both. It rises out of hope rather than despondency.

The Contrite Heart

Contrition is God-centered, which is considering the hurt to Him, rather than self-centered, which consists of sorrow for oneself. Contrition ends in salvation, whereas attrition leads to reprobation. True sorrow of heart results in a permanent change of mind rather than a superficial change from which one may easily lapse. It is a transformation rather than a conformation.

Let us return to David. In his penitential Psalm he pleads for mercy and lovingkindness. He requests cleansing from his iniquity and his wicked heart. He acknowledges his transgression and admits that his sin is ever before him. He states his faith in the ordained means which is the sprinkling of blood by hyssop, and he looks forward in faith to the sense of forgiveness and cleansing, after which he will be able to teach transgressors the Divine way. Then, in summary, he cries out, "Thou desirest not sacrifice; else would I give it: thou delightest not in burnt offering. The sacrifices of God are a broken spirit: a broken and a contrite heart, O God, Thou wilt not despise." David spoke out of his sorrow because he had sinned against the God who loved him and blessed him in an unusual way. That was true contrition.

Josiah succeeded the wicked Manasseh as king of Judah. He inherited the customs which were contrary to the Divine pleasure. One day they brought to him a copy of the law which had been found in the rubbish of the Temple. It was read to him. When the king heard the words of the law, he rent his clothes and declared the beginning of a reform throughout Judah. To him came the Divine response, "Because thine heart was tender, and thou hast humbled thyself before the Lord, when thou heardest what I spake against this place, . . . and hast rent thy clothes, and wept before Me . . . behold, therefore, I will gather thee to thy fathers, and thou shalt be gathered into thy grave in peace; and thine eyes shall not see all the evil which I will bring upon this place." That was true contrition.

Jesus' closest friend failed Him in the hour of His need. He denied Him thrice in the courtyard of Caiaphas' hall. Peter was sure that he would want nothing more to do with Christ, but just then Jesus passed by, being led from the judgment hall, and looked at Peter. All of the former love of a deep and true emotion welled up from the depths of Peter's heart when he realized what he had done against Jesus. We read that he went out and wept bitterly. Peter was sorry that he had wounded Jesus by his action. That was real contrition.

On the cross there was a hardened criminal who was suffering the due reward of his iniquity. He had no fear of temporal punishment. He had suffered the worst, and as for the future he was ready to take his chance with that, too. But as he hung on Calvary, he saw something that broke his heart. He saw One suffering innocently, regally, lovingly and forgivingly, and out of his broken heart he cried, "Lord, remember me when Thou comest into Thy kingdom." That was true repentance.

Evidence of contrition rests in three things. First, a confession of one's sinfulness. David said, "Against Thee, Thee only, have I sinned." The thief said, "We receive the due reward of our deeds." The second evidence is that of prayer. This prayer is not only for the forgiveness of one's sin but for the cleansing of heart. David said, "In sin did my mother conceive me ... create in me a clean heart, O God." The third evidence is that of heart obedience to the Scriptural command. Jesus said, "If ye love Me, keep My commandments." This desire of heart to obey is a clear indication of the beginning of love.

III. THIS GODLY SORROW OF HEART SHOULD RESULT IN CONVERSION.

Paul wrote concerning this godly sorrow, "Behold ... what carefulness it wrought in you, yea, what clearing of yourselves, yea, what indignation, yea, what fear, yea, what vehement desire." This contrition produces a change in one's life. It is a powerful instrument brought to bear upon the affections, and it results in conversion.

Conversion is the translation of a Greek word into English (by way of the Latin), which means repentance. *Con* is about, *verto* is to turn. It means a total change of heart and life. This includes the renunciation of sin. It is a radical breaking with every known form of sin. Such a renunciation arises from the realization of what sin means to God and what it cost Him. Conversion is attended by a hatred of sin. Jesus never hated sinners. He simply drove out their sin when they would permit Him. The converted man receives from Jesus this same hatred of sin. Conversion also results in humility. "Humiliation is of two kinds, legal and evangelical,"

Jonathan Edwards said. "The former may be exercised while we are in a state of nature, the latter is peculiar to the saints, and consists of the sense they have of their own utter insufficiency, despicableness and odiousness, with an answerable change of heart . . . this frame of mind is given in evangelical humiliation only, in which the inclination is changed by a discovery of the holy beauty of God. In legal humiliation the conscience is convinced, but the will is not bowed nor is the inclination altered. In legal humiliation men are brought voluntarily to deny and renounce themselves: in the former they are subdued and forced to the ground: in the latter they are brought sweetly to yield and do delight to prostrate themselves at the feet of God." With this agree the many words of the Scripture such as, "He giveth grace to the lowly"; "Blessed are the poor in spirit for theirs is the kingdom of God"; and, "Verily I say unto you, whosoever shall not receive the kingdom of God as a little child shall not enter therein."

Conversion, arising out of true contrition, is God-given. Paul advised Timothy to instruct those in error with a meek spirit, hoping that "God peradventure will give them repentance to the acknowledging of truth." God instigates, man co-operates. It is from the spiritual influences of conviction that man is brought to contrition. Only in those through whom effectual grace is operative does repentance reach its final state in conversion.

Conversion, then, is a laying hold of Divine mercy.

The Contrite Heart 69

The message of repentance is a message of wrath, clearly illustrated by the work of John the Baptist, but implied in it is the great truth of a loving Father who sent Jesus to bear our sins in His body on the tree. There never could have been a complete conversion on the part of man, a changing from wickedness to righteousness in life habits and from the power of darkness unto light in the mind, without the coming of God into the world to remove that sinfulness. The atonement of Calvary was a basic essential to the message of repentance. The scene of Calvary should be the means of breaking the hardened heart of sinners.

Jesus was contrite of heart. At the conclusion of His private ministry with His disciples, He came into the garden of Gethsemane. To the two sons of Zebedee and Peter, who went farther than the rest with Jesus, He said, "My soul is exceeding sorrowful even unto death." Jesus' heart was breaking because of sin, because of what sin was to entail on the morrow. Jesus yielded up unto God the most perfect contrition for sin. It was an infinite contrition. Because of this some have erroneously concluded that the sorrow for sin yielded to an offended Deity was the essence of the Atonement, since it revealed justice in operation in a Divinely governed universe. But this contrition of Jesus was not sufficient for the salvation of the sinner. It was necessary for Him to die to make satisfaction for sin. It is also necessary for the individual to experience a personal contrition which will lead to his change of mind toward Christ and his active faith in that vicarious satisfaction of Jesus for his salvation. We earnestly desire to point all hearts to Him who carried their sins that they might manifest a true sorrow because their sins were against God. This will lead them to real salvation.

V.

THE BELIEVING HEART

"If thou shalt confess with thy mouth the Lord Jesus, and shalt believe in thine heart that God hath raised Him from the dead, thou shalt be saved. For with the heart man believeth unto righteousness."
—ROM. 10: 9, 10.

THE act of believing is commonly known as "Faith". The believing heart designates the life of faith. When Peter replied to the question, "What shall we do?" which was asked by those who were pricked in heart, he gave a two-fold answer. He said, "Repent and believe on the Lord Jesus Christ." We have considered repentance in the form of contrition for one's sin. The other form of repentance is that of conversion, or active righteousness. Contrition, as we saw, is true godly sorrow for sin because of its effect upon God, not for the consequences which we suffer because of it. Conversion includes both a turning from sin and an active belief. Therefore, it is rightly subsumed under the study of "The Believing Heart." We now come to consider the act of belief. This, likewise, includes two things. There is the belief which means faith, that is, the act of trust, of resting one's confidence in a person, and there is also the life according to that faith. "To believe" originally meant to live according to something. This active aspect of faith is too often neglected. Jesus preached, "Repent ye and believe the Gospel." He meant: "Have a confident trust in Me and live according to what I have told you."

Faith is the prominent doctrine of Bible Christianity. Faith, as such, was lost when works became substituted for it. This tendency first manifested itself in the New Testament Church under the leadership of men who were called Judaizers. They admitted that it was necessary for a man to have faith in Christ in order to be saved, but they held it was also necessary for him to keep the law as best he could. Salvation, according to them, was not by faith alone and not by works alone, but by faith and works together. The Judaizers held that a man's obedience to the law of God was not sufficient for salvation, but that it became sufficient when it was supplemented by Christ. Against this compromise, the Apostle Paul insisted on salvation by faith without the works of the law. Either Christ was able to save a man or He was *not* able. There could be no compromise. Due to Paul's strenuous efforts, the Judaizers were expelled from the early Church, but they did not cease their activities. They caused the apostle a tremendous amount of trouble in the Galatian and the Corinthian churches. The tendency and doctrine of salvation by faith and works gradually came to dominate sections of the church until today it is exactly the thing that is being taught by the Roman Catholic Church.

In the later Middle Ages faith was emphasized less

The Believing Heart 73

than works, and as a result religious people were attempting to earn their salvation by all manner of religious works. The story of the reclamation of faith from this moral debris of self-righteousness which had accrued about the true attitude of faith through the years is connected with Luther. In the Rathaus at Erfurt a series of friezes beautifully depict the important stages in this great conflict. First, Luther is seen as a student, singing his way through school. The handsome lad is depicted standing before the home of Frau Cotta when, as a begging student, he earned what he could to support himself in school. It was as a result of this that Frau Cotta took him into her home, where he stayed for three years, while he continued his studies. The scene gives the impression that Luther was a normal German lad of the Sixteenth Century.

The second frieze reveals Luther deciding to be a monk. He had left Eisenach to study law at the University of Erfurt. After he had finished his undergraduate work and was beginning his legal studies in earnest, a sudden change came over him. While walking in the forest a storm arose and during this storm Luther felt compelled to dedicate himself to be a monk. Later, his friends attempted to dissuade him. His father was disappointed. He left the halls of the beautiful university and went to the black cloister of the Augustinian monastery.

The third frieze shows Luther in a cell of the black cloister, flagellating himself with a scourge until he fell insensible. Here among the monks for seven years Luther sought peace of soul by faith and works. He prayed through the long nights. He made pilgrimages. He practiced asceticism. All to no avail. For long hours he poured over the Scriptures but finally, through the suggestion of an elderly monk and the teaching of the book of Galatians, Luther realized that "the just shall live by faith." The scales fell from his eyes and he gave himself to the exposition of the two great books of the New Testament which proclaim justification by faith, namely, Romans and Galatians.

The fourth frieze depicts Luther in a rough wagon, stopping to preach to the crowds which gathered round him when he journeyed to the Diet of Worms. Before this, he had found peace in his own soul and had become professor in the University of Wittenberg. His ideas had become opposed to those of the Church hierarchy. He had nailed his theses to the door of the church at Wittenberg. He had preached against the selling of indulgences in Saxony. He had burned the Papal bull and he had advanced rapidly toward a break with Rome. The picture attempts to catch him in the attitude with which he answered the Emperor's summons to be tried for his heresy at the Imperial Diet. Luther was acquainted with the dangers and with the fate that had enveloped his predecessor, John Huss, a century before. It was a dramatic trial, ending with Luther's replying to those who asked him to recant his views, "I cannot retract; God help me. Amen." That was the birthday of the Reformation and it came to pass because of the ordeal of a soul which had sought salvation through faith and works and had found peace with God through faith alone.

The Believing Heart

Acknowledging that justification by faith is one of the three primary doctrines of Protestantism, we nevertheless accuse ourselves as Protestants of misusing this doctrine. There has been a tendency on our part to confine faith to the body of beliefs, rather than to include the active confidence in Christ as our Saviour and the resultant conversion of life arising from this confidence. This has not been true with the great Protestant theologians or in the great Protestant revivals, but it is a tendency in the attitude of the average Protestant believer. Our purpose here, then, is to examine the subject of faith so as to find in it the full Scriptural content resulting in salvation.

In that superb passage concerning faith contained in the eleventh chapter of Hebrews we are told what faith is. The writer says: "Without faith it is impossible to please Him: for He that cometh to God must believe that He is, and that He is a rewarder of them that diligently seek Him." This tells us that faith is founded on knowledge, is the expression of a creed, and rests in a person. Faith has been defined as "a firm conviction wrought in the heart by the Holy Spirit as to the truth of the Gospel, and a hearty reliance on Christ for salvation." This is true Christian faith which must have as its foundation the truth of God's faithfulness and the truth of the Word of God which tells us of His faithfulness.

We shall limit our discussion to: first, The Object of the Heart's Belief; second, The Experience of the Believing Heart; and third, The Proof of the Believing Heart.

I. The Object of the Heart's Belief—The Faith.

Our text says: "If thou shalt confess . . . Jesus." The ultimate Person in whom our faith rests as an object is God, but the immediate object of our faith is Jesus Christ. When we state the creed, we say, "I believe in God . . . in Jesus Christ . . . and in the Holy Ghost." Now in order to have trust in a person we must know something about that person. Faith is never founded upon ignorance, but upon knowledge. We are aware that there is a widespread emphasis upon the attitude of faith rather than the object of faith. This emphasis says that it does not make any difference what or in whom one believes as long as one believes. We are told that it is the attitude of faith which heals and stimulates and sustains. This emphasis is disparaging to the intellect in religion. It is impatient with all attempts at definition of terms and insistence upon creeds. It urges a unity of all men who are at all religious, regardless of what they believe. This we feel to be utterly opposed to the Christian religion. Whenever any of the Biblical writers attempted to stimulate faith on the part of their constituents in Jesus they were always careful to tell something about Jesus. This was true of Peter's Pentecostal address, when he clearly proclaimed the Deity, humanity, the atonement and the judgeship of Christ. It was true of Paul's addresses when he declared at Antioch and at Athens that the human Jesus was man's Saviour, that God had raised Him from the dead, that through Him is preached the forgiveness of sin, and that, finally, He would judge

The Believing Heart

the quick and the dead. John, the Beloved, plainly states that "whosoever believeth that Jesus is the Christ is born of God," that "he who believeth that Jesus is the Son of God overcometh the world," and that "he who believeth on the Son of God hath the witness in himself." Peter, in his first Epistle, added that "unto you which believe He is precious." There is utterly no meaning to the statement that we may have faith in Jesus or may love Jesus if we do not know something about Jesus.

Our text states the two most important things that we are to believe about Jesus. First, we are to believe that He died, and second, we are to believe that God raised Him from the dead. When Paul refers to these two events in the tenth chapter of Romans, it is with the understanding that we have followed him through the previous statements in the same Epistle concerning Jesus. He had dealt very fully with the meaning of Jesus' death. He had informed us that whereas by the deeds of the law no flesh can be justified in God's sight, for all have sinned and come short of God's glory, we may be "justified freely by God's grace through the redemption that is in Christ Jesus, whom God set forth to be a propitiation through faith in His blood, that we might have remission of sins," and that "God might be just and the justifier of him which believeth in Jesus." This is a clear statement of the atonement which involves the way in which Jesus saves us from sin. Thus we see that faith requires a theology. It involves the committing to Him of our immortal souls, which may be justified only by an appeal to the facts.

Those facts about Jesus are given in the Scriptures. They form a theology. There we have His lofty claim to be regarded as the eternal Son of God who came voluntarily to the earth for our redemption, who manifested His glory in the days of His flesh and who carried the guilt of our sins in His body on the cross. This is the meaning of Jesus' death.

But we are not to stop here. We need to know that Jesus is alive. Hence, we must know something about the Resurrection. There is such a thing as the unbelief of joy, such as that manifested by the ten disciples who saw Jesus in the upper room. It says, "While they yet believed not for joy," He spoke to them. It was too good to be true, but the unbelief of joy was gradually dissipated and the joyous belief in the Resurrection was established by the infallible proofs of the open tomb and of Jesus' resurrection appearances. The disciples, themselves, believed that Jesus was living. It is this fact of Christian history concerning Jesus which, becoming part of the knowledge of the believer, enables Him to have confidence in Christ as his Saviour. Paul had written in an early chapter of Romans, "Abraham's faith was imputed to him for righteousness," and "This was written for us also to whom it shall be imputed if we believe on Him that raised up Jesus our Lord from the dead, who was delivered for our offenses and was raised again for our justification." This, then, we must know about Jesus, that He died for our sins, that He rose again from the dead, and that He is living. One thing is clear about the New Testament account of Jesus' own words and of the testimony about Him: Jesus presented Himself not merely as an example of a believing heart, but as the object of faith. He not only invited men to have faith in God like His own faith in God, but He invited them to have faith in Him as the Messiah, as the heavenly Son of Man who was to come from glory and to be the instrument in judging the world.

Our text states yet one other imperative which is to be the object of our faith concerning Christ. Paul says, "If thou shalt confess with thy mouth Jesus as Lord." Here is the personal faith in Jesus' Lordship. Of course this involves His Deity, His Messiahship, His Saviourhood, and His present Kingship, but it means more than that. It means a personal yielding unto Jesus as Lord of one's own life. If we believe in Jesus as Lord, it means that we have accepted Him as our Lord. This is the main purpose of the Gospel of John, namely, to stimulate faith in men's hearts concerning Him. The key says: "These things are written, that ye might believe that Jesus is the Christ, the Son of God: and that believing ye might have life through his name." Quickly review in mind the great events recorded in John's Gospel. There was the testimony of John the Baptist in order that they might believe that He was the Lamb of God who taketh away the sin of the world. There was the conversation with Nicodemus telling of the necessity of the new birth, through faith in His death, that whosoever believeth might not perish but have everlasting life. There were the various miracles of healing and of raising the dead, that the disciples and others might believe that He was the Son of God. There was the promise to those who believed upon Him that they would never hunger and never thirst, and that they would have a well of spiritual life within them from which rivers of living water should flow. There was also the promise that whosoever believeth in Him, though he were dead, yet shall he live, and whosoever liveth and believeth in Him shall never die. These and numerous other incidents and promises were recorded by John that men might believe in Jesus as the object of their faith. The believing heart places its confidence in the Person of Christ.

II. THE EXPERIENCE OF THE BELIEVING HEART— JUSTIFICATION.

The hub of all Christian doctrine is justification by faith. It is linked with sin, with the atonement, with regeneration, and with righteousness. We are led to believe that all Christian doctrine stands or falls with this one doctrine and, therefore, we are not ashamed to proclaim it even in this day. The doctrine of justification is not an involved and intricate thing. It is very simple. It is simply the Bible answer to that eternal question of the human soul, "How shall I become right with God?" There are only two answers to that. One answer is, by keeping the law of God perfectly. That is a good answer, but men have found through the ages that if this is the only way of salvation, they are lost. The rich young ruler believed that he kept the law, but yet felt that he lacked something in order to possess eternal life. The defect in this method of salvation is that no man except Jesus ever obeyed God's law perfectly. Hence, the law becomes an instrument of condemnation. Because we have failed to obey, we deserve death, exclusion from the household of God, and the just punishment of our sins. Is there, then, no other means of salvation? Happily there is. The Bible tells us that the guilt of our sin was laid upon Christ and that He died, instead of us, on the cross, that the demands of the law, both as to punishment and obedience, have been fulfilled and the terror of the law is removed. In the eyes of God we are justified. We are clothed with Christ's righteousness and we may stand without fear even as Christ stands without fear before the judgment bar of God. Our guilt was imputed to Him and His righteousness was imputed to us.

The Westminster Confession of Faith thus defines this experience: "Justification is an act of God's free grace, wherein He pardoneth our sins and accepteth us as righteous in His sight, only, for the righteousness of Christ imputed to us and received by faith alone." It is a judicial, objective, single and complete act whereby God as Judge declares the believer to be righteous. In this justification the sinner, through faith, is identified with Christ in His death and in His resurrection. Through faith he has taken his position on the cross whereby he died unto sin and he has shared with Christ the resurrection from this death into a new life of righteousness. Now the Bible teaches that we are justified by faith. This leads some to believe that justification must depend upon an act of man as well as upon God, but faith does not consist in doing something, it consists rather in receiving something. Justification by faith is simply another way of saying that we are saved solely by the One in whom our faith is reposed. Faith is the instrument, the means, the point of contact through which salvation is received. The Bible does not say that we are saved on account of our faith but through our faith. The Bible doctrine is salvation by grace. Thus to say that we are justified by faith is to say that we cannot save ourselves in the slightest measure, but that God saves us. The efficacy of faith rests upon the object of that faith, namely, Christ. Moreover, to more clearly reveal that this is not a work of man, the Bible even represents faith itself as a work of the Spirit of God. The believing heart is passive in the experience of justification.

The other side of justification is regeneration or the new birth. Whereas justification is a forensic and declarative act, regeneration is a creative act of God. It is defined as: "That act of God by which the principle of the new life is implanted in man and the governing disposition of the soul made holy." This new birth is a change of man's nature, of his heart. It is wrought by the Holy Ghost. Ruskin said, "The reason preaching is so often ineffectual is that it calls on men to look for God rather than behold Him working for them."

In the justified life, the act of believing brings God's blessing. It is by faith that we are able to do the works which Jesus expects us to do. He said, "He that believeth on Me, the works that I do shall he do also; and greater works than these shall he do; because I go to My Father." Faith also is the source of the answer

The Believing Heart

to our prayers. Jesus said, "All things whatsoever ye shall ask in prayer, believing, ye shall receive." He said, "Whatsoever things ye desire, when ye pray, believe that ye have received them, and ye shall have them." The believing heart also becomes the source of the religious affections for, reverting to our first text, we read: "Whom having not seen ye love; in whom, though now ye see Him not, yet believing, ye rejoice with joy unspeakable and full of glory."

III. THE PROOF OF A BELIEVING HEART—GOOD WORKS.

The Bible declares three times that "the just shall live by faith." We have seen that works alone, or works and faith, merely condemn. It is grace alone which saves, but works do have a place in the discussion of the believing heart. There are those who would make love the instrument of salvation. They would say that we are saved by love. In one sense that is true. We are saved by the love of God manifested in Christ's redeeming acts, but no believer is saved by his own love. Jesus did not say to the woman, "Thy love hath saved thee, go in peace." He said, "Thy faith hath saved thee." But works of love have a very definite and important place in the Christian religion.

Concerning this, there is an apparent contradiction upon first reading the epistle of Galatians and the epistle of James. In the first, Paul says, "A man is not justified by the works of the law, but by the faith of Jesus Christ." James says: "Ye see, then, how that by works a man is justified and not by faith only." Because of this apparent contradiction Luther, in the throes of his great conflict with the Church of Rome, refused to give the epistle of James a place in the canon. Later, he came to see his error and spoke of it highly. How are we to reconcile these two statements? First, we must remember that James was probably the earliest book of the New Testament. It was written before the terms "faith" and "works" became established in their meaning, before the rise of the Judaistic controversy. Therefore, upon analysis we find that James uses the word "faith" in a different sense from that in which Paul uses it. James makes clear when he speaks about the demons who also believe and tremble, that He is referring to a faith which is merely intellectual, one that involves only an apprehension of certain things as facts. This intellectual faith is essential to salvation but it is not sufficient for salvation. One may give assent mentally to the facts presented in the Bible and yet not accept the gift of salvation which is offered by Christ. The exercise of the act of confidence by which one trusts Christ is saving faith. That is the faith which Paul speaks of. Intellectual faith may be followed by a life of sin, but this is inconceivable in the Pauline sense. James was simply stating that intellectual faith was insufficient for salvation and that the whole nature of man must be changed. Paul says that same thing by telling us that we are justified by faith and that faith works through love. Love is the fulfilling of the whole law.

The Christian life in this world is not passive but is active. When Habakkuk said, "The just shall live by his faith," he used the word meaning "faithfulness."

Jesus said, "All things are possible to him that believeth." The entire eleventh chapter of Hebrews, calling the roster of the heroes of faith, gives evidence to this faithfulness. By faith Abel's sacrifice was accepted. By faith Enoch pleased God and was translated that he should not see death. By faith Noah was warned concerning the flood. By faith Abraham became the father of a nation. By faith Moses became the deliverer of the Israelites. By faith Joshua possessed Canaan. "What shall I say more? For the time would fail me to speak of Gideon, and of Barak, and of Samson, and of Jephthah, of David also, and Samuel, and of the prophets, who through faith subdued kingdoms, wrought righteousness, obtained promises, stopped the mouths of lions, quenched the violence of fire, escaped the edge of the sword, out of weakness were made strong, waxed valiant in fight, turned to flight the armies of the aliens . . . of whom the world was not worthy." Believing manifests itself in faithfulness. We believe and therefore we speak and act.

When Paul made his defense before Felix he said, "This I confess unto thee, that after the way which they call heresy, so worship I the God of my fathers, believing all things which are written in the law and in the prophets." Because Paul believed he was willing to face the opposition of the Jews, the persecutions of Rome and the obstacles which came in his path. Faith for him was the source of his action.

We may believe or not believe, but Jesus knows which are believing hearts. John said of him: "Jesus knew from the beginning who they were that believed not." A believing heart leads one unto salvation for the Gospel is the power of God unto every one that believeth. Unbelief ends in a hardened heart. "For this cause God shall send them strong delusion that they should believe a lie: that they all might be judged who believe not the truth."

One of Jesus' last pleas was concerning the believing heart. Thomas had been absent when Jesus first appeared to the disciples in the upper room. He said, "Except I see in His hands the print of the nails and put my fingers in the print of the nails and thrust my hand into His side I will not believe." The second time Jesus appeared, Thomas was present. Jesus showed to him the evidences of His suffering and of His resurrection and said to him, "Reach hither thy finger and behold My hand; and reach hither thy hand and thrust it into My side: and be not faithless, but believing." We repeat that Scripture—"Be not faithless, but believing. If thou shalt believe in thine heart that God hath raised Him from the dead thou shalt be saved, for with the heart man believeth unto righteousness."

VI.

THE HARDENED HEART

"The Holy Ghost saith, Today, if ye will hear his voice, harden not your hearts, as in the provocation, in the day of temptation in the wilderness: when your fathers tempted me, proved me, and saw my works forty years. . . . "
—HEB. 3:7-9.

THE only alternative to repentance and faith is unbelief. One has said, "Unbelief is the child, not of the head, but of the heart . . . if unbelief were the creature of our intellect we must needs meet it there with argument; but since it is the product of a wrong state of heart, of an evil heart, we must meet it there." William Law said that it is an eternal truth that reason always follows the state of the heart, and what the heart is, that is the reason. If the heart is full of sentiment, of penitence, and faith, the reason will take part with the heart; but if the heart be shut up in death and dryness, the reason will delight in nothing but dry objections and speculations.

Our text is a warning against this attitude of heart, taken from the culminating book of New Testament revelation—Hebrews. The writer quotes from a Davidic Psalm words which he attributes to the Spirit of God. Four hundred and fifty years after the wilderness wanderings of the children of Israel, David, in the Spirit, admonished the men of his day not to harden their hearts as did their fathers in the provocation. The writer of Hebrews takes this same eternal truth and applies it to the men of the first century as vividly as did David to the men of his day. Hence we may accept the warning for ourselves concerning the possibility of refusal to believe. Spurgeon said, "Fickleness is bound up in the heart of man, unbelief is our besetting sin . . . this is no mean offense, and will bring with it no small punishment." It is well to be warned concerning it.

The writer of Hebrews reverts to the Old Testament in the midst of his treatise upon the nature and office of Jesus Christ in order to obtain a vivid illustration of what happens when one refuses to believe on Him. He rehearsed the situation of the children of Israel which resulted from their turning back at Kadesh Barnea, and instead of entering Canaan, the land of promise, they were compelled to wander in the wilderness for forty years. You remember the story. With mighty wonders and a high hand God had delivered the Israelitish slaves from their taskmasters in Egypt. The waters of the Red Sea had been parted to permit them to cross and then had rolled back upon the pursuing Egyptians, bogging their chariots and horses and ultimately overwhelming them. Above them during the day was a fleecy cloud in the blue sky, ever present to guide them in their journey. At night that cloud was as brilliant as fire. When their provender was exhausted, God fed them with the food of angels, the manna. He brought water forth from the rock. He even caused quails to be carried by an east wind into the camp that they might have meat. Now they arrived at the border of the promised land, the land of rest and plenty. God had said, "I will give it unto you. I will go before you and drive out the inhabitants of the land and will give it to you for a possession." Instead of believing God, the tribes insisted on sending spies in to view the land. They wanted to know for themselves whether it was a good land and whether they were able to take it.

The returning spies divided, because of disagreement over their report, into two committees, a majority and a minority. Ten of the spies reported favorably concerning the land but advised that the inhabitants were too strong for the Israelites to take it. Two of them accurately reported on the condition of the land and its inhabitants but they said, "God is able to deliver it into our hand." The multitude of the Israelites, however, accepted the report of the ten, trembled with fear, murmured against Moses for bringing them out of Egypt to die in battle, and decided that they would not enter the land. Their attitude and action was one of unbelief. They rejected the promise and protection of God, thereby provoking and grieving Him. All of the subsequent wanderings and evils which the children of Israel suffered during the next thirty-seven years directly arose from this great act of unbelief.

An indictment of Israel's unbelief and subsequent hardness of heart is contained in the Seventy-eighth Psalm. There it says, "They kept not the covenant of

God, and refused to walk in His law; and forgot His works, and His wonders that He had showed them . . . they sinned yet more against Him by provoking the most High in the wilderness. They tempted God in their heart by asking meat for their lusts, yea, they spake against God . . . they believed not in God, and trusted not in His salvation . . . their heart was not right with Him . . . oft did they provoke Him in the wilderness, and grieve Him in the desert . . . a stubborn and rebellious generation; a generation that set not their heart aright, and whose spirit was not stedfast with God." Moses had characterized them as obstinate, stiff-necked, rebellious and obdurate. The record shows that these words were accurate.

Unbelief is the direct cause of hardness of heart. Our Scripture says, "Take heed, brethren lest there be in any of you that evil heart of unbelief, in departing from the living God." An evil heart is the source of unbelief and unbelief results in greater hardness of heart. Let the heart fall into an evil state, harboring sinful things which it would not excuse in others but condones in itself, embracing unrighteous thoughts and desires, and immediately such a heart will find it difficult to believe in God. Infidelity arises from man's disinclination to retain God in his knowledge. Best is it to cultivate the good heart. Jesus' strongest words of condemnation are found where He upbraids men for their unbelief and their hardness of heart. It is a psychological law that we can harden our hearts, but we cannot soften them. Unbelief is the direct means to this end.

I. THE PERSON WHO HARDENS THE HEART— THE AGENT.

This topic is one which demands the attention of the mind in its entirety for if only one angle of the subject is grasped and another one is missed, it may result in irretrievable harm. To illustrate let me say, God is the primary agent in hardening the heart. Paul says: "Therefore, hath He mercy on whom He will have mercy, and whom He will He hardeneth." Now pause. This is not the end of the matter. Even the Confession of Faith says, "The doctrine of this high mystery of predestination is to be handled with special prudence and care." It is not our purpose to deal with God's part in hardening hearts or the subject of reprobation. We have done this on other occasions. Sufficient is it to know that "God from all eternity did by the most wise and holy counsel of His own will, freely and unchangeably ordain whatsoever comes to pass; yet so as thereby neither is God the author of sin nor is violence offered to the will of the creature, nor is the liberty or contingency of second causes taken away, but rather established." God does all things. He says, "I am the Lord, and there is none else. I form the light, and create darkness. I make peace, and create evil: I the Lord do all these things." Nothing in the world can come to pass without God's power. The Bible says that all things are accomplished by God, yet so that liberty remains for the creature. It is distinctly taught by James that God cannot be tempted with evil, neither tempteth He any man. God is good and holy and righteous, with whom there is no variableness neither shadow of turning.

This Hebrew conception of God as the first cause, supreme and unaffected in His being has sometimes obscured the truth about second causes. Let me illustrate: Paul quotes the book of Exodus by saying that God hardened Pharaoh's heart. He was considering primary causes, yet in the same chapter we read, "and Pharaoh's heart was hardened," while in the next chapter the same narration says, "But when Pharaoh saw that there was respite he hardened his heart." Pharaoh refused to believe God's warnings and His promises, and he hardened his heart; ultimately, however, in the sense that God is the cause of all things, God hardened Pharaoh's heart. John gives the same interpretation to the words of Jesus. He is telling of the visit of certain Greeks to see Jesus. In Jesus' response He told them the necessity of His death. The Jews questioned the claim Jesus made to the Messiahship. Jesus replied, "Yet a little while is the light with you. Walk while ye have the light, lest darkness come upon you." John then commented that while He had done so many miracles before them yet they believed not on Him because the Scripture said concerning Israel, "He hath blinded their eyes, and hardened their heart; that they should not see with their eyes, nor understand with their heart, and be converted, and I should heal them." The Semitic mind does not demand the delicate distinction needed by the Occidental mind between first and second causes.

The other side of predestination is man's freedom.

Says The Confession, "God hath endued the will of man with that natural liberty, that it is neither forced, nor, by any absolute necessity of nature determined to do good or evil." Jesus said unto the Jews, "Ye will not come to Me that ye might have life." We have the knowledge that we possess this freedom. Evidence of it exists in the smiting of conscience, when we have violated the sense of oughtness, in the feeling of responsibility, and in the dilemma of alternating choices. We know that we are free to believe or not to believe. That freedom does not mean that we are at liberty to act contrary to our nature, for the only reason why we do some things rather than others is that our choice comes out of our nature. God alone by His grace can enable man freely to will and to do that which is spiritually good, by translating him from darkness to light. But at the same time we have the consciousness of freedom—freedom, according to the evil disposition of our nature, or freedom according to the good disposition of our nature. Moreover, the Bible places guilt and blame upon those who do not believe. These are two sides to the same great truth. Both are presented in the Scripture and both are found in life. We must leave their final harmony to the knowledge of God, and our apprehending of it to the time that we shall know as also we are known.

The immediate agent in hardening the heart is the individual. We may speak with great certainty when we deal with second causes. The text says, "harden not your hearts." Direct agency is attributed to the individual in this experience. Again we must revert to the Israelites. This hardening took place by their refusal to believe God's Word. God accused them of tempting Him or trying Him ten times. They made tests of His goodness. Their lack of trust was a slur upon God Himself. No one who values his veracity can endure to be suspected, mistrusted, and derided when there is no ground for it. Especially when he has been the agent of great blessings and mercies. Such a practice within the marital relationship would inevitably end in trouble. One who has given ample evidence of love through many years would be greatly grieved by any test of his affection, but this is exactly what the Israelites did. They forgot God's mercy, His blessings and faithfulness of the past and they tested Him to see if He would be faithful in the future. Then they added to their unbelief overt sins such as murmuring, complaining, and rebellion, so that He was deeply grieved. They heard the word as it was preached, but our author says, "It did not profit them, not being mixed with faith." Constant hearing without faith on the part of an individual is culpable.

These Israelites also refused to act on God's Word. This was the essence of their provocation. They disobeyed Him. God's faithfulness was sufficient to warrant their implicit trust and obedience. Instead, they set up their self-will against God's Revealed Will. They knew the better but they did the worse and thus they provoked Him. They were the direct agents in their heart hardening.

This practice on the part of individuals is sometimes known as choosing God's permissive will rather than His decreed will. Of course, that does not mean the decreed will in the sense that it must come to pass, but in the sense of the higher and the lower. When one refuses God's best he takes the second best. God permits a man to harden his heart and thus God hardens it. This does not affect the total Divine plan for the universe, for it must be embraced within it, but it condemns the individual who chooses this way. God's plan is neither changed, deferred, nor conditioned by the individual. Whether you conform to it or not, distinguishes between a tender and a hard heart. As we shall soon see, the only way of entering into God's rest is by perfect submission to His will.

II. THE PROCESS OF HARDENING THE HEART.

Once again we must refer to a passage of Scripture which is avoided constantly by Bible expositors. It is in the eleventh chapter of Romans. Paul was answering the question as to whether God has cast away His people because of the fact that Israel had rejected Christ. This he denied by presenting himself as an example of the Jews who believed. Then he argued that God always has a remnant, as He did in the days of Elijah when every true believer was persecuted by Jezebel and Ahab, who worshipped Baal. Said Paul, "Even so then at this present time also there is a remnant according to the election of grace. And if by grace, then it is no more of works: otherwise grace is no more grace. But if it be of works, then it is no more grace: otherwise, work is no more work. What then? Israel hath not obtained that which he seeketh for; but the election hath obtained it and the rest were hardened." The translators of the authorized version, fearful of the word "hardened," translated it "blinded." But Thayer defines the word, "To grow hard or callous, become dull, lose the power of understanding."

This is a quotation from Isaiah. It is confirmed by the words of David. God gave them the spirit of slumber, eyes that they should not see and ears that they should not hear. Thus the writers of the Bible agree that as far as Israel was concerned it was within the plan that there should be a temporary blindness or hardening in order that the Gospel might go unto the Gentiles, but the plan also included an ultimate redemption even of Israel, for Paul adds, "If the fall of them be the riches of the world, and the diminishing of them the riches of the Gentiles; how much more their fulness?" Temporarily Israel has been visited with insensibility, or torpor of mind, so that it is not nationally affected by the offer made of salvation through the Messiah, but some day that dullness will be removed and they shall yet be a blessing to the world. This is merely another illustration of the same truth which we have been examining.

How does Paul describe the process of this hardening? He uses the form of ossification of the nature of man. The figure is of a broken bone exuding liquid substance around the fracture, which becomes jell-like and then solidifies into bone. Such he says is the condition of man's nature in the process of hardening. This is biologically sound. An article in the Atlantic

Monthly entitled, "The Philosophy of Growth" says that there are three physical stages in life, the liquid, the jell and the ivory. With plants there is first the watery stage, then the bud and then the wood. The same is true of animals. In the history of an individual, he passes through juvenescence, maturity and sinescence. This would correspond to childhood, youth, and age. A little child without any difficulty can put his feet behind his neck. Later, he finds such contortions difficult. Thus it is with the mind. In the first stage, people can learn very rapidly. In the second stage, they have the power of initiation. They originate ideas. In the third stage they are merely tombs. It takes only a few years toward the close of life for many to enter into the ivory state. The struggle of life is to keep the mind in the jell stage until the end. God help us, if when we are young or middle-aged men, we enter the ivory stage mentally.

If this is true in the physical and the psychological, why should it not also be true in the spiritual? Youth is very impressionable to the concepts of God and duty and responsibility. By far the majority of all conversions take place in the teen age. Let that softness and tenderness of heart once pass by and be followed by the stiffening experiences of life and it is not long until ossification begins. Remember that the hardest heart was soft once and the softest may get hard. "The chalk which now holds the fossil of shells was once moist ooze. The horny hand of toil was once full of soft dimples. The murderer once shuddered when, as a boy, he crushed a worm." The religious affections are the function of man's nature most quickly influenced by this hardening process.

Hardening begins when man rejects the offer of Christ as Saviour. Israel's blindness came when it refused to accept Jesus Christ. First the Pharisees and the people enthusiastically thronged about Jesus. Then they resented His violation of their customs, and they grew to hate Him because He revealed their sinful hypocrisy. It was a gradual experience, but when Stephen preached to them concerning this Jesus, and unhesitatingly spoke of their action toward Him, they were cut to the heart, they gnashed upon him with their teeth, and they stoned him unto death. Thus also Paul found them in his missionary labors throughout the Mediterranean world. From his Roman prison came the word recorded by Luke at the close of Paul's life: "Well spake the Holy Ghost by Isaiah the prophet unto our fathers, saying, Speak unto this people, and say, hearing ye shall hear, and shall not understand; and seeing ye shall see, and not perceive: for the heart of this people is waxed gross, and their ears are dull of hearing, and their eyes have they closed; lest they should see with their eyes, and hear with their ears, and understand with their heart and should be converted, and I should heal them. Be it known therefore unto you, that the salvation of God is sent unto the Gentiles, and they will hear it."

Our Scripture says that hardness comes through the deceitfulness of sin. Judas was probably once a tender and impressionable lad with great possibilities. Otherwise, he could never have had a place in the apostolic

The Hardened Heart

band. He saw all the miracles of Jesus. He heard the teaching. He came under the sweet, loving influence of that incomparable Christ, the same influence that summoned forth the love of the other disciples. But Judas did not believe, he considered in his heart the delights of sin, and gradually his unbelief and his sin deceived him by hardening his heart and making him a traitor.

The one phrase which would probably designate mankind, today, more than any other is hardness of heart. Merciless killing in war, ruthless liquidation of political enemies, cruel removal of competitors in business regardless of the lives quenched thereby, inconsiderateness of human feeling in divorce where children are orphaned, indifference to the Gospel of Christ wherein God's love has been demonstrated and impenitence for the grossest acts of sin, these are all but manifestations of the hardness of heart which is written across the faces and into the very language of mankind.

III. THE PENALTY OF HARDNESS OF HEART.

Unbelief brings a terrible penalty. Says the Scripture, "So I swear in My wrath, they shall not enter into My rest." Unbelief treasures up the wrath of God. Paul says, "Despisest thou the riches of His goodness, forbearance and longsuffering; not knowing that the goodness of God leadeth thee to repentance? But after thy hardness and impenitent heart treasurest up unto thyself wrath." Unbelief in a God who has manifested such attributes as goodness, forbearance and longsuffering is the clear evidence of a hard heart. This merits

the Divine wrath. The Israelites had turned back out
of unbelief and were condemned to die in the wilderness. Their carcasses fell in the desert. Sand was their
shroud. The procession was a funeral march through
the desert. It took thirty-seven years for the last one
of that generation to perish, but until that one was gone
Israel could not enter God's promised rest. Their murmuring and complaining and departure from God
brought them under the judgment of a righteous being.
Why one should exchange the rest of the cool shade
tree for the scorching heat of the noonday sun, or the
beautiful summer for the north winds of winter, or
the plenty of Canaan for the scarcity of the wilderness,
is more than we can understand, but it is the penalty
of unbelief.

Unbelief excludes one from God's rest. Though the
Israelites did not enter, the Scripture says, "There re-
maineth therefore a rest to the people of God." What
is this rest which is so needed in the mad rush of
a machine age marked by the collapse of mind and
body and spirit? The Scripture says it is God's rest.
Now what is God's rest? God entered His rest following
the six creative days. The seventh day commenced His
Sabbath. It is an endless, imperturbable, unlimited experience of Sabbath keeping. Within it all creation
spends its years as a tale that is told. This rest is not
one of inactivity, for God is sustaining by His power
this great universe which He created and is working
out our redemption. Now this is the rest which we are
invited to share. It is not the sleep which comes after
exhausting toil, nor the indolence of inactivity, but it

is the calm peace of God in the midst of strenuous living and of taxing toil. Paul describes it as the peace which passeth understanding. The Christian's experience in Christ is his Canaan. Christ is the promised land that flows with milk and honey and where the new corn of Divine life may be eaten. To be made partaker of Christ and of His unsearchable riches is to have entered into God's rest.

There is a paradox here, for the Scripture says, "Let us labor, therefore, to enter into that rest." It also says, "For we which have believed do enter into rest." The Christian life is a struggle to overcome sin, temptation and unbelief daily in life. This struggle will never be fully ended until we pass beyond this bourn of time and place, for our ultimate rest is heaven. Yet in a very true sense we enter that rest now and are seated with Christ in the heavenlies where we share with Him the joys, triumphs, and glories of His resurrection-ministry. No one of unbelief shall enter into this sanctified life.

Missing God's rest condemns one to the wilderness experience. The wilderness is a place of suffering, of struggle and of pain in a religion of works without the grace of God. It has all the unrest of aimless, unsatisfied wanderings, of striking one's tents only to pitch them again in another place that looks just like the one which you recently left. Here there is nothing of the freshness, the unending newness, of the hills and valleys in the Canaan of God's imperturbable rest.

I am Shammua. I am of the tribe of Reuben, the strength of Jacob. Let me tell you my story. I was a

slave in Egypt and suffered terribly from the lash of
my taskmasters, from the toil of my work and from
anxiety over my loved ones. I gladly followed Moses
and Aaron with the Israelite host out of Egypt. I
saw the waters roll back. I saw the cloud separating
us from the Egyptians and later leading us in the
wilderness. I drank of the bitter water which was
sweetened at Marah. I ate of the manna and of
the quail. I heard the rumblings of Sinai and saw
Moses come down with the tablets of the law. I
spied out the land of Canaan and saw the walled cities
with their vineyards and their forests and their farms.
I wandered in the wilderness because I was one
of those who murmured, and who turned back. I recall
how bitter my heart was against Moses and Jehovah
when I saw a comrade stricken by the sun or bitten
by a fiery serpent or fallen from the plague. I was
one of the last of that generation to go. Loneliness came
over me, and solitude. I wanted to turn to God, to believe as once I did, to live until we should enter the
promised land, but alas, I, too, finally died in the matter
of Peor wherein thousands of the children of Israel
were slain. My life was hard. My heart was bitter.
I rued the day when I failed to believe in the living
God who can save. Let me speak to you now. Today,
if ye will hear God's voice, harden not your hearts
as in the provocation, in the day of temptation in the
wilderness when we tempted Him and proved Him . . .
labor to enter unto God's rest. Take heed lest there be
in any of you an evil heart of unbelief.

VII.

THE BURNING HEART

"Did not our heart burn within us, while He talked with us by the way, and while He opened to us the Scriptures?"
—LUKE 24:32.

FOLLOWING our pause to consider the alternative to a believing heart, we now return to the direct progression of our series of discussions. Our considerations have included the facts of depravity, of conviction, of repentance, of faith and of unbelief. The faith which we proclaimed had its object in the Person of Christ and His atonement and resurrection, which compose the central facts of Christianity. We are not justified in elevating the death of Christ above His resurrection or His resurrection above His death. They are of equal importance, but it is our purpose to stress the doctrine of the resurrection just now. The death of Jesus as an atonement will be discussed when we speak of "The Pierced Heart."

"If Christ be not risen our preaching is vain and our faith is vain." This doctrine is essential to the faith and hope of every Christian. It is the most certain fact in the history of Christianity. The resurrection is substantiated by logical, historical and psychological evidence. Because of this it is the fundamental apologetical argument of Christianity. The reality it carries with it substantiates all the main claims of the Christian religion. By it Christianity may be proved and when it is proved it becomes a reasonable religion, satisfying the highest laws of logic. If the resurrection were not true it would impugn the other great truths of Christianity. It is inseparable from the belief in the trustworthiness of the New Testament Scriptures, for they clearly teach it. It is inseparable from the trustworthiness of Jesus for He based His claims to Deity upon this event. It is inseparable from the teaching of the atonement of Christ for His death, though a great martyrdom, would have been valueless if He had remained in the tomb. It is inseparable from the Christian doctrine of immortality, for Christ's resurrection is a pledge and pattern of our own resurrection, and finally, it is inseparable from the doctrine of the second coming, for if Jesus is coming again, He must possess a glorified body.

It is not our purpose, however, to present the arguments for the resurrection, great as they are, and the benefits derived therefrom. Rather, it is our purpose to depict the experience that accompanies faith in the resurrection and the experience which accompanies a lack of faith in the resurrection.

The incident which forms the basis to our discussion happened on the first day in which Christ rose from the dead. It is the fourth appearance of Christ after His death and burial. There are eleven appearances of Jesus in resurrected form recorded in the New

Testament narratives. Most interesting are they when surveyed in order.

On the resurrection morning, which was the first day of the week, a group of women went to the tomb with aroma and spices with which to anoint the body of Jesus. One who has seen a tomb at least similar to the tomb of Christ, if not the actual one, can never forget it. At twilight one summer evening I found my steps turning to the garden near Gordon's Golgotha where is located the reputed tomb of Christ. There, about a hundred yards from the hill, resembling a skull, is a quiet garden tended by an old Englishman. One is admitted after a declaration of his purpose and allowed to wander among the olive, fig and eucalyptus trees and along the little paths of the flower garden. The garden was cool for the hot Syrian sun was dropping into the Mediterranean. Taking my seat just opposite to the tomb, the whole scene became vivid once more. There was the great stone in its groove which could be rolled backward and forward, opening and closing the tomb. There was the small aperture above the door through which the sun could pour its morning rays. Inside there was a long, carved resting place for the body. By stooping one might enter. This particular tomb was discovered some years ago, after Gordon decided that the hill of the skull was possibly Calvary. It was piled high with bodies of Crusaders and on the floor was a great red cross painted in blood. Whether this is the actual tomb of Christ's or not, one cannot say, but it certainly filled every demand of the Scriptural conditions.

In the place near where I was sitting, the women came and rested over against the tomb, while Joseph laid the body away before Nicodemus arrived with the embalming spices. It was the purpose of the women on the morning of the resurrection to perform the same service which Nicodemus and Joseph of Arimathæa had performed opon their departure and before the sealing of the tomb. When they arrived on the resurrection morning, they found the tomb opened and an angel sitting upon the stone at the door. He said, "Fear not ye: for I know that ye seek Jesus, who was crucified. He is not here: for He is risen as He said. Come, see the place where the Lord lay. And go quickly, and tell His disciples, that He is risen from the dead."

Mary ran to announce the fact to Peter and John and the women returned to the city. While on the way they met the risen Christ, and Mary, having returned to the garden, also caught a vision of Him, at first thinking Him to be the gardener. He said, "Why weepest thou?" In anguish she replied, "If you know where they have taken Him tell me and I will take Him away." Then said He, "Mary," and with the words her eyes were opened and she recognized her Lord as living.

During that same day He appeared to Simon Peter, with the purpose, no doubt, of healing him from his backsliding. Toward the evening of the resurrection day, He appeared to Cleopas and his friend on the road to Emmaus. Late that night the risen Christ manifested Himself to the disciples who had secreted themselves behind closed doors, Thomas being absent.

The Burning Heart 107

One week later He appeared to them again in order that Thomas might be there. The seventh appearing was to the conference of all believers, called at a mountain rendezvous in Galilee where Jesus delivered the great missionary commission. He appeared again in Galilee at a quiet lake from which He had called His chosen three. Later, at the close of the forty-day period, He walked out to the Mount of Olives with the apostolic group, instructing them to wait for the promise of the Holy Ghost, when He was suddenly taken away from them. Two other appearings are recorded, one to James, the brother of the Lord, and the other to Paul, after the ascension of Christ.

It is the fourth of these in which we are interested. Two disciples were walking from Jerusalem to Emmaus, a distance of about eight miles to the west of Jerusalem. The road passes the tomb of the kings, the old city of Mizpeh, and reaches Emmaus just before it turns into the valley of Ajalon. They were talking as they walked. The conversation concerned the recent happenings at Jerusalem. Suddenly, a stranger joined them in their journey and asked them about their conversation. They must have talked together for several hours for the same journey took a group of us three hours on horseback because of the roughness of the going. After the good man joined them, the center of the conversation turned about him. He rebuked them for not believing the Scriptures and then explained to them the teaching of Moses and the Psalms and the prophets until these recent happenings. The time passed rapidly and they soon arrived at

Emmaus. The interesting stranger would have gone on had they not urged him to stay and partake of the evening meal with them. While they reclined at the table He began to break bread. They stared at Him and were startled. They recognized Him. They looked at each other to confirm it and then back at Him, but lo, He was gone. They leaped to their feet, excitedly discussed his vacant place and confirmed in their minds that it was the Risen Lord, saying, "Did not our heart burn within us, while He talked with us by the way, and while He opened to us the Scriptures?" Then said they, "Let us return and report it to the disciples." At Jerusalem they found that the same excitement was there, for the Lord had appeared to Peter, and all of them knew of it.

From this story there are three outstanding facts for us to note. First, the disciples had lost the glow of the burning heart. Second, there was a reason why they had lost the glow. Third, the glow returned when their eyes were opened spiritually and when they were convinced of the resurrection.

I. THEY HAD LOST THE GLOW OF THE BURNING HEART.

Translating literally, Cleopas said to Jesus, "We had hoped that it had been he who was about to redeem Israel." They had possessed that hope but now it was gone. They were hopeless and despairing following the resurrection.

The glow of the burning heart had been theirs during their fellowship with Jesus. They had known the glow of service. Many of us find that in our good

The Burning Heart 109

works we have a burning heart. A young preacher used to testify, "Every now and then I become depressed and unhappy. Then I immediately look for some good I can do for someone and as soon as I do it I find that my burden leaves me." There is much truth in this. When those disciples had been serving with Jesus, healing the sick, feeding the poor, and preaching the Gospel of the kingdom to all comers, they experienced the glow of the burning heart.

They had felt the fire that had been kindled by the teaching of Christ. Their hearts burned within them as they listened by the grave of Lazarus when He said, "I am the resurrection and the life," and on Solomon's porch during the last week when He said, "I am the vine and ye are the branches . . . My glory is as the glory of the Father." What blessed hours were those when they heard the Sermon on the Mount from the Horns of Hattin, when from Olivet they learned of events of the future in reference to Jerusalem, and when the Old Testament was revealed through the words of their Master.

They had been consumed with anticipation when they thought of the kingdom. Truly they had a mistaken notion of that kingdom based upon Jewish apocalyptic ideas, but the thought of the kingdom itself was true. There was to be a kingdom, one now in joy, peace, and righteousness in the Holy Ghost and one in glory to come. Their hearts leaped wih joy at this thought.

They also had the passion of witnesses. They had seen the miracles, they had talked with Lazarus after his resurrection, and they had glimpsed the glory of Jesus on the mount of transfiguration. Could anyone have been with that Person long without catching the glow from Him? They accepted what He said and were acting on it. They believed Him and He gave them power. Was it possible that during this the shine was missing? No, they beamed and sparkled for God.

They also had the added impetus of fellowship one with another. When a dozen burning fagots are bound together a hot fire is kindled. If one can chase a thousand, two can chase ten thousand. Remember Gideon's three hundred. It was some such power and glow that these twelve and the seventy had experienced when in fellowship with the Master and with each other.

But alas, most of this ended like the burst of a bubble. It was like the enthusiasm which ran riot in England in the eighteenth century and which ended in that financial catastrophe called The South Sea Bubble. It was not unlike our own prosperity days before 1929. When they ended the people came to earth with a bump. Similarly, the disciples came to themselves with a thud. They realized that their ideas of the kingdom were false and that they were now without a king. They found that their glow was the glow of an enthusiasm and was not founded upon fact and understanding. It was an awful shock. One thing great soul winners have always guarded against is wild enthusiasm. They know that when people meet the hard, cold temptations of life after an enthusiastic religious experience or a meeting, the shock often causes a reaction. We have witnessed this in the case of temporary

The Burning Heart   111

conversions. People receive the word with gladness but the shocks are too great for them to endure.

This glow had not the foundation that was necessary to stand the persecution which was bound to arise against those who held to the teaching of Jesus. They had not thought that through. Their loyalty was too shallow as yet. They needed to be brought to the earth. This was clearly shown by the way they retreated from Jesus at the time when He needed them most. All of them fled and Peter denied Him.

Then came the shock, the catastrophe. Jesus was siezed, tried, mocked, scourged, crucified, and buried. There was no disputing it. He was dead. He who was to redeem Israel from the yoke of Rome, He who was to set up a Jewish kingdom, He who was to be their spiritual and material deliverer, was dead. With one blow the enemy had broken their hopes and shattered their fondest plans.

They were as sheep without a shepherd, scattered abroad. The fire of their zeal was out, or at least was burning very low. There was nothing but a smoldering reminiscence of what had been and what they hoped would be. Some few were in Jerusalem, the women and the ten. Most of the others had already turned their faces toward their ancestral homes and work. It was a dismal, lifeless, broken, hopeless company that made up that scattered flock of which Cleopas and his friend on the road to Emmaus were representative.

II. THE CAUSE OF THE LOST GLOW.

Just before they had left Jerusalem the report came from Mary Magdalene and the other women that Christ was not in the tomb, that He had appeared to them. Scorning it, they left on their journey, but it sufficed to reopen the topic for discussion. Suddenly from a small side road a stranger of humble but attractive bearing appeared. After saluting them, He said, "What manner of communications are these that ye have one with another, as ye walk and are sad." The interruption offered the opportunity to discuss the matter further. Cleopas said, "Art thou only a stranger in Jerusalem, and hast not known the things that are come to pass there in these days?" And he told him of Jesus of Nazareth, His life, His works, miracles, His ignominious death, and of their hope and how it had been blasted, and now of the report of the women, but that it was hard to believe.

Then said the stranger, "Oh fools and slow of heart to believe all that the prophets have spoken. Ought not Christ to have suffered these things, and to enter into his glory?"

When God calls a man a fool he is indeed a fool. Only the man who says in his heart that there is no God, the man who lives for this world alone and the man who turns from the truth are fools. But these men were called fools by the risen Christ of glory. Why? Because of their unbelief. They were slow of heart to believe. They knew what the prophets had said and they had heard from His own lips how that

He must suffer and then enter into glory, but they were so filled with their fond ideas of an earthly kingdom that when the Scriptures were fulfilled and His own words had come to pass, they refused to believe it. Such a man is a fool. What fools there are in the world today! They not only have this evidence but all the added evidence of the resurrection and of historic Christianity, and yet they refuse to believe that He is the One who is to redeem Israel.

This impertinent stranger then proceeded to expound the Scriptures. He produced evidence that this man Jesus was the Christ. He began with Moses, who wrote, "The sceptre shall not depart from Judah, nor a lawgiver from beneath his feet, until Shiloh come ... binding his foal unto the vine and his ass's colt unto the choice vine; He washed his garments in wine, and his clothes in the blood of grapes." Moses also wrote, "The Lord thy God will raise up unto thee a prophet from the midst of these thy brethren, like unto me; unto Him shall ye hearken." David, in the second Psalm said, "Yet have I set my king upon my holy hill of Zion; I will declare the decree: the Lord hath said unto me, Thou art my son, this day have I begotten thee." Again in Psalm forty-five he said, "Thy throne O God is forever and ever: the sceptre of thy kingdom is a right sceptre," and in the twenty-second Psalm the words which Jesus appropriated on the cross, "My God, My God, why hast thou forsaken Me?" In the 110th Psalm was the teaching which Jesus appropriated during his last week to confound the Pharisees. David had said, "The Lord said unto my Lord, sit Thou

at My right hand, until I make Thine enemies Thy
footstool." David had called his son his lord.

In the prophets are many references to Christ which
the stranger brought forth. Isaiah spoke of the virgin
who would conceive and bear a son and call his name
Immanuel. Of Him he wrote, "For unto us a child
is born, unto us a son is given: and the government
shall be upon His shoulder . . . He shall be called
the everlasting Father, the Prince of Peace." This
exalted individual was to be a servant. "Behold my
servant, whom I uphold; mine elect, in whom my
soul delighteth: I have put My Spirit upon him:
he shall bring forth judgment to the Gentiles . . .
his visage was so marred more than any man . . . he
is despised, and rejected of men; a man of sorrows
and acquainted with grief . . . He was wounded for
our transgressions, he was bruised for our iniquities:
the chastisement of our peace was upon Him and
with His stripes we are healed." Jeremiah wrote, "The
days shall come, saith the Lord, that I will raise unto
David a righteous Branch and a King shall reign and
prosper and shall execute judgment and justice in the
earth. His name is the Lord our righteousness." Daniel
added, "And the Messiah shall be cut off, but not for
Himself; and the people of the prince that shall come
shall destroy the city and the sanctuary." Zechariah
is probably the most definite of all. He said, "Behold
thy King cometh unto thee: He is just, and having salvation; lowly, and riding upon an ass, and upon a colt
the foal of an ass. . . . The Lord said unto me, Cast it
unto the potter; a goodly price that I was prized at of

them. And I took the thirty pieces of silver, and cast them to the potter, in the house of the Lord." These are only a few of the prophecies to which Christ must have referred as being fulfilled in His life and death. Now imagine one for the first time having this explained to him by the risen Lord. When Cleopas and his friends understood, is it any wonder that their hearts burned within them? They were taught by Christ. That is the way our hearts should burn within us when we are taught by Him through the Scriptures, today.

III. THE RETURN OF THE GLOW OF A BURNING HEART.

The little group continued on its way to this beautiful town of Emmaus, where the wonderful stranger would have left them had they not urged Him to stay. How little did they know as yet whom they were to entertain. The Scriptures say that some have entertained angels unawares. Remember the experience of Abraham, of Gideon and of Manoah. Often we may miss a great blessing, perhaps the greatest we would ever receive, by our inhospitality. Priscilla and Aquila found their greatest blessing in the entertainment of Paul. The book of Philemon is a veritable monument of hospitality. At Emmaus they found lodging and began the evening meal. Without hesitancy they requested him to break the bread and give the blessing. He was accepted as one of them. Then it was they recognized Him and He disappeared.

Up until this time their eyes had been holden. They had not understood the great truths in the Word of God nor had they recognized Christ. They deserved the rebuke for not believing the Scriptures, but the reason for their slowness during this time was that Christ had not been with them since His death and the Holy Spirit was not yet given in His fullness to interpret the Word to them. If our eyes are holden today so that we do not perceive spiritual things there is one of two reasons at the base of it, either we are not yet Christians and the Book is closed to us or else we are slow to believe what we have learned because we do not have the Holy Spirit in His fullness.

As soon as their eyes were opened they experienced the burning glow. Their first words were, "Did not our heart burn within us while He walked with us by the way?" They did not realize the true import of the burning heart till they saw it in relation to Christ. Unless all of our experience is connected with Him, the glow is only enthusiasm. No matter how enthusiastic our aim may be, if our prayers are not connected with the Christ in glory, the glow is not there. Do we experience that intense burning upon the fires of our heart when we are in prayer? We should. Without that passion of Christ, prayer is only a dull spiritual exercise. Where is the flame that should leap from the pages of Holy Writ to kindle again our desire for holiness and righteousness through reading of the Word of God daily? How many of us read out of duty or read not at all! If we had burning hearts, these passages of comfort would be the voice of God to us daily, directing our ways and meeting our needs; it is that burning heart which will drive us out after times of communion to serve. Have we a heart burning with sympathy for our brethren? Do we see the heathen without hope when we rest in our knowledge of salvation? Does our heart burn with the message of salvation without which the world is dying? If so, it will move us to action as it moved the prophets of old. A heart like that is a dynamo not to be stilled.

The disciples immediately returned to Jerusalem to tell the apostles who were still there. Darkness, bandits and robbers had no terror for them. They were aflame with the love of Christ. What a conversation theirs must have been! They almost ran along the way. Their hearts were ready to burst with joy.

That is the kind of experience we ought to have—one that glows with and for God. It puts a polish upon our countenances. It puts a song in our hearts. It puts a message upon our lips and it puts wings to our feet. We become true children of God, manifesting His glory. Jeremiah of old said, "His Word was in my heart as a burning fire shut up in my bones, I was weary with forbearing, and I could not stay." Our Christ and our Gospel are the Gospel and the Christ of the burning heart. May faith in the death, burial, and resurrection of Christ cleanse us from our sins, make us new creatures in righteousness and fill us with His Holy Spirit that the fire of His love may burn upon the altar in the shrine of our personality.

VIII.

THE PURE HEART

"Blessed are the pure in heart for they shall see God."

—MATT. 5:8.

PURITY depends upon the Holy Spirit. To be convinced of the resurrection of Jesus from the dead is not enough for true religion. One's heart must be purified. The believer must be cleansed from secret sin. David prayed this prayer: "Who can understand his errors? Cleanse Thou me from secret faults. Keep back thy servant also from presumptuous sins." And Moses wrote, "Thou hast set our iniquities before Thee, our secret sins in the light of Thy countenance." Secret sins are of two kinds, those which are secret to us and those which are secret to others, or to put it another way, those that we try to hide or those that are hidden from us. In either case they constitute unrecognized sin. Sins which sometimes are hidden from us are attitudes which we assume of arrogance described by the phrase "better than thou," of pride which is sometimes spiritual and of wilfulness in relation to others. We may not even recognize that we have these sins and yet almost everyone else who knows us recognizes their presence in our lives. Sins which are hidden from others and secret to ourselves may be such as ambition,

The Pure Heart

covetousness, envy, anger, impatience and even intemperance. Believers may be aware that these exist in their lives and yet be successful in hiding them from other people. They are secret sins.

Sins like these must have been confessed by the disciples in their ten-day prayer meeting before Pentecost occurred. It was necessary for them to realize that these sins were present in their lives, that they were contrary to God's will and that it was necessary to make a clean breast of them. They already were convinced of the resurrection, but they did not receive complete purity of heart until they faced the presence of these things.

It is necessary for one to be purified from vacillation in Christian living. James says, "Cleanse your hands ye sinners and purify your hearts ye double-minded." Only purity of heart can give singleness of purpose. Many of us need to pray for deliverance from this in the words of the hymnist Robert Robinson:

"Oh to grace, how great a debtor,
Daily I'm constrained to be!
Let thy goodness, like a fetter,
Bind my wandering heart to Thee.

Prone to wander, Lord, I feel it,
Prone to leave the God I love;
Here's my heart, oh take and seal it;
Seal it for Thy courts above."

The believer needs also to be purified from his habit of seeing people, events and things as ends in themselves. The pure heart is one which sees God in humanity, in the events of history and in the details of daily life. This vision of God in and back of and through all of life is an evidence of the pure heart.

To be cleansed in heart necessitates the high office work of the Holy Spirit in sanctifying power. We must first recognize that the Holy Spirit is a Person, or a center of Divine consciousness. The Bible always speaks of Him as such. It attributes personality to Him, referring to Him in the personal pronoun and ascribing to Him all the powers of personality such as willing, speaking, being grieved and being the author of free action. We must recognize that He has all the attributes of Deity. As God He is infinite in His Being, in His power, in His wisdom, in His love, in His holiness and in His truth. The Spirit is God in action in the world today. He is the agent of the Triune God in the work of redemption as it continues now. The Spirit's work is defined by Jesus as the convicting of sin, of righteousness and of judgment. The Spirit restrains the processes of evil in the world and prevents sin from being totally destructive of human life. The Spirit applies the great truths concerning God, the redemption in Christ Jesus and judgment to come on the basis of the moral law to the hearts of men. But the Spirit also works for righteousness in the heart of believers by purifying them. This is not the least of His works. It is the preparation of an elect people through their existence in this world for a sinless and glorious existence in heaven. He begins that work of purification now that men may begin to see God in this

The Pure Heart

life and be ready to see Him at the conclusion of the world when they pass on to the world to come. This process is known as sanctification.

To be Christian in heart, or to have sanctified affections, demands purity by three means: first, Purity by the Blood of Jesus; second, Purity in the Holy Spirit; and third, Purity through Christian Purpose.

I. PURITY BY THE BLOOD OF JESUS—CALVARY.
THE PAST.

Before we may speak about sanctification, it is necessary to recognize the guilt, corruption and bondage of past sins which demand that we be purified from them. Theologians who wrote the Confessions of the Church defined sin and declared what its consequences are. Sin itself was a transgression of or want of conformity to the majestic law of God. Sin brought all mankind into a state of misery, suffering and death, both physical and spiritual. These definitions of sin and its effect have little influence over the minds of men. Only by tracing the experience of sin in life through blasted romance, tearful separations, funeral processions and acute suffering, can we know what sin actually is. The great novelists cause these experiences of life to move vividly before us. It is easy to talk about adultery, but only when one reads Tolstoi's Resurrection and follows the consequences of the one act of Nehludof and Katusha through the sorrows and griefs which directly arose out of it does he catch the meaning of sin in this form. Talking about the guilt of sin is like reading the hard cold narrations of the historical period of the Judges without seeing the relation of the national lapses into idolatry and bondage to the individual family life of the people, but when one turns to the book of Ruth and finds a simple Hebrew family emigrating because of the famine brought on by these invasions to a land where death and sorrow awaited them as exiles, he catches something of the heart beat of these facts in every day life.

We might choose but two illustrations from individual lives of the past year. One is a young woman. She came because she had no one else to whom to go, and she confessed her wrong doing, her sense of guilt and corruption, and her fear of the consequences. With tears burning their way down her cheeks she told the story and awaited words that might bring her hope for purification. It was the old story of the guilt of sin. The other which we arbitrarily choose is a young man caught in the throes of habit, suffering the bondage of past sin. Shamefully he told of Christian parents and of fine home rearing and of his own unworthiness. Then with the earnestness of his plea written into his depressed but wistful eyes he asked for some help from the Christian religion. He merely represented the tens of thousands who are chained in similar bondage to some sin but who do not have the courage to seek help through the Christian religion. The past demands some means of purification.

The only means available in all human experience for the cleansing of past guilt and corruption and for the breaking of such bondage is the blood of Jesus as it was shed on Calvary. "Be it known unto you that there is none other name under heaven given whereby we must be saved." Eloquently does the simple Gospel song express that fact.

> "What can wash away my sin?
> Nothing but the blood of Jesus!
> What can make me pure within?
> Nothing but the blood of Jesus!
> Oh, precious is the flow
> Which washed me white as snow,
> Precious is the blood of Jesus."

The numerous blood sacrifices of the Israelite religion foreshadowed the effectual blood of Christ as a means of salvation. The blood of Jesus was not emphasized in the Hebrew-Christian religion because of this sacrificial background. In the revealed Judaistic-Christian tradition there is no remission of sin except by the shedding of blood. This we are told is because the life is in the blood and on Calvary the blood of the God-man Jesus was shed for us by which a satisfactory substitution was made for guilty man in bearing the penalty of sin.

The Bible expressly declares that the blood of Jesus cleanses us from past sins. Paul said that God set forth Jesus Christ to be a propitiation through faith in His blood to declare His righteousness for the remission of sins that are past, and that being justified by His blood we shall be saved from wrath through Him. In the epistle to the Ephesians we are explicitly informed that we have redemption through His blood, the forgiveness of sins, according to the riches of His grace. By the blood of Christ we who were afar off are made nigh, we who were at enmity with God are made at peace. An entrance into the very Presence of God has been accomplished for us by it and that blood has sanctified us as the people of God. The New Testament Church is referred to as the flock purchased with Christ's own blood. Blood has such a part in the cleansing of sin that the great assembly around the throne of God was foreseen by John as singing a new song saying, "Thou art worthy to take the book, and to open the seals thereof: for thou wast slain, and hast redeemed us to God by Thy blood, out of every kindred, and tongue, and people, and nation."

The very communion, the most precious service of worship in the church, represents the blood of Jesus shed for many for the remission of sins. Thus the Scripture says, "The cup of blessing which we bless, is it not the communion of the blood of Christ? The bread that we break, is it not the communion of the body of Christ?" Thus Jesus said, when He took the cup and had supped, "This cup is the New Testament in My blood: this do ye, as oft as ye drink it, in remembrance of Me."

It is the act of believing that Jesus shed His blood on behalf of the sinner that cleanses one from sin. The Bible attributed this cleansing to two factors. One is expressed by the efficacy of the blood in the text: "If we walk in the light as he is in the light, we have fellowship one with another and the blood of Jesus Christ his Son cleanseth us from all sin." The other emphasizes the efficacy of faith in which the Scripture declares that the hearts of the Cæsaræan Christians were purified by faith. These may be combined by saying that the purifying process from past sins takes place through faith that the blood of Jesus was shed for sin. Peter summarized it at the apostolic council when he said, "Men and brethren, ye know how that a good while ago God made choice among us that the Gentiles by my mouth should hear the word of the Gospel, and believe, and God, which knoweth the hearts, bare them witness, giving them the Holy Ghost, even as He did unto us; and put no difference between us and them, purifying their hearts by faith." Thus it was that the house of Cornelius received the forgiveness of past sin.

II. PURITY IN THE HOLY SPIRIT—PENTECOST— THE PRESENT.

The guilt of our sin is cleansed by the blood of Jesus, but the present purity of our experience is effected by the Holy Spirit. The Holy Spirit enters the heart which has been purified by the blood. Peter said that God witnessed that their hearts were purified by faith by giving them the Holy Ghost. The Holy Spirit enters the heart of the believer to unify it in mystical life with other believers in the body of Christ. We are all baptized by one Spirit into one body. The communion of that body of Christ should keep one pure. We are told in a recent history of American religious culture that the Christians of Calvinistic background in this country approached the Lord's Supper with deep reverence and with great emphasis upon

Paul's word about taking care that the believer does not eat and drink the body and blood of Christ unworthily. Sometimes I think that the present Church approaches the communion in too light and glib a fashion. Though we would not return to the days of the tokens used for admittance to the communion yet we would enjoin the practice of keeping ourselves pure as we approach the table. If the Holy Spirit has not entered a heart at conversion the experience was merely reformation rather than regeneration. The new birth of the sinner into the body of Christ can take place only by the effectual operation of the Holy Spirit.

To retain and enjoy this present experience of purity the heart must be yielded to the Holy Spirit. There is a difference between receiving the Holy Spirit at our conversion and being filled with the Spirit through consecration. Paul says, "Yield yourselves unto God as those that are alive from the dead, and your members as instruments of righteousness unto God." It is only by absolute submission unto the will of God that the Spirit may constantly fill and constantly cleanse your heart. God never asks man's cooperation. He demands man's submission. Here wilfulness enters as sin. Here the harboring of secret sins causes the defiling of the believing heart. These sins must be completely yielded unto God. In order to do that there must be a consecration of one's entire being. It is not necessary that consecration should be deferred a long time after one's conversion. The normal experience of a Christian would seem to be an immediate consecration of his powers and his person-

The Pure Heart

ality unto the agent of the Godhead upon conversion. Tragic it is that so many Christians cease with being cleansed from past sins in their experience of God's power. It is not enough to remove the penalty. We must experience the power, the power of the indwelling Spirit of God.

The condition of the abiding Presence of the Holy Spirit in his constant cleansing power is obedience— implicit, unquestioning obedience. During the second persecution of the early church, Peter testified to the Sanhedrin of the saving work of Jesus Christ in His death and resurrection and then added, "And we are witnesses of these things; and so is also the Holy Ghost, whom God hath given to them that obey Him." It was the obedience of the apostles in the early Church that guaranteed to them the conscious presence and supernatural power of the Spirit of God in their work. The heart may know the purity of the Spirit's Presence by being permanently yielded unto Him.

Such a pure heart enjoys the constant vision of God by the Spirit's work. If we would see God, the best place to behold Him is on Calvary. There His justice, mercy and love were manifested in their fullness. There in the face of Jesus, who though knowing no sin was made sin for us, is mirrored our sin both in its past guiltiness and in its hidden form. God hath set them forth there in the white light of His countenance. Now the Spirit of God takes the things of Jesus and shows them unto us. Jesus said that when the Spirit would come He would speak of Him. The Spirit will show us God reconciling the world unto

Himself in the wonder of Calvary. Moreover, because the spirit Himself is God He makes God's presence real within us. God is no longer afar off. He is immanent within us. Life itself then takes on a new meaning for God saturates existence itself with His Presence. Such is the privilege of a pure heart.

III. Purity Through Christian Purpose—Separation. The Future

We can not stop in our thought concerning the pure heart without mentioning its sustained purity. This becomes a matter of separation from evil which is one of the meanings of sanctification. Heart purity may be lost through grieving the Holy Spirit. Paul warns us to grieve not the Spirit of God whereby we are sealed against the day of redemption. Any kind of indulgence in sin, any root of bitterness springing up in the heart, any failure to purify oneself from the evils of the flesh is grieving unto the Spirit of God. This is commonly known as backsliding and I suppose most of us are more or less in a backslidden state if we have ever known what it means to be filled with the Holy Spirit. For this reason we are commanded to be separate. Said Paul, "Be not unequally yoked together with unbelievers; for what fellowship hath righteousness with unrighteousness? and what communion hath light with darkness? and what concord hath Christ with Belial? or what part hath he that believeth with an infidel? . . . wherefore come out from among them and be ye separate, saith the Lord, and touch not the unclean thing." The process of sanctification progresses by separation from evil. Positively, however, sanctification proceeds by following the leading of the Spirit. Said Paul, "If the Spirit of him that raised up Jesus from the dead dwell in you, he that raised up Christ from the dead shall also quicken your mortal bodies by His Spirit that dwelleth in you . . . for as many as are led by the Spirit of God, they are the sons of God." God's Spirit will guide us into truth and righteousness and light.

Heart purity is never a once for all experience, but it demands a daily effort. We are to reckon ourselves as dead unto sin. This means a constant considering ourselves as crucified with Christ. In other terms of the Scripture, we bear in our body the dying of the Lord Jesus. Such an end to the old man or to the former deeds of the unregenerate nature demands a mortification of the desires of the flesh, a laying aside of all deeds of evil. Where failure to reach this perfect standard occurs there must be the daily cleansing of the blood of Jesus which is a constant process.

Heart purity thus may be retained only by the purpose not to defile ourselves. When Daniel was taken into the king's court at Babylon he saw the existence of the wise men and the courtiers in their luxury and loose life and he determined that he would not defile himself. This determination was pursued at a great cost. He jeopardized the favor which he had won with the king's chamberlain, he endangered his possible standing in the court by absenting himself from the feasts of the king and he made himself the object of the ridicule of the other favorites of the king, but Daniel was determined to carry out his purpose. The consequence of this separation from defilement and his practice of devotion was that Daniel was blessed above others. He was blessed in health and in wisdom and in position in the king's court. The king learned by experience that God was with Daniel in all that he did. Heart purity retained by such a purpose is rewarding in every-day life, but the Scripture says that the chief purpose of heart purity is the hope of the coming of Jesus Christ. "For he that hath this hope purifieth himself even as He is pure."

Our text proclaims that the man of pure heart is blessed because he shall see God. Let the vision of God be your blessed experience. The consummating reward of Daniel's purpose to remain pure was a vision of the Christ and a revelation of what Christ would do for His people and for the world. He saw God. Our vision of God may be a present experience in the commonplace of life and we may hold forth the hope of seeing Him visibly in the presence of Jesus, yet either of these demands heart purity. When Isaiah saw the corruption of his nature, he cried out, "Woe is me! for I am a man of unclean lips, for mine eyes have seen the King." Then one of the seraphim flew with a live coal from off the altar and touched his lips, saying, "Lo, thine iniquity is taken away and thy sin is purged." Once we have been purified of our sins let us retain our purity through the indwelling Spirit and a Christian purpose.

"Finally, brethren, whatsoever things are true,

The Pure Heart

whatsoever things are honest,
whatsoever things are just,
whatsoever things are pure,
whatsoever things are lovely,
whatsoever things are of good report;
if there be any virtue,
and if there be any praise,
think on these things."

IX.

THE TROUBLED HEART

"Let not your heart be troubled: ye believe in God, believe also in me."

—JOHN 14:1.

THE troubled heart describes a soul at grips with the problems of life. It is as common a mental and spiritual condition as is heart trouble a physical condition. In fact, both kinds of trouble are on the increase. In the decade from 1920-1930 the number of deaths recorded from heart disease increased at some ages nearly fifty per cent. This, we are told, was partly due to the fact that other fatal diseases were conquered by medicine and more people survived until the heart wore out and partly, also, to the fact that as the knowledge of the heart increased, many deaths were recognized as from heart disease which had hitherto been attributed to some other cause. Then, also, heart trouble increased from the rapid tempo of modern life. With this increase in troubles of the heart a new interest has developed in the mechanics of the heart. Charles Lindbergh and Dr. Alexis Carrel, in collaboration, have invented a mechanical heart which in time may have some influence on the diseases of the heart at an early stage in life. The increase in both troubled hearts and heart trouble is due to a disturbance at the seat of

The Troubled Heart 133

man's personality, his affectional region. Modern life has unbalanced the functioning of the nature of man. So much so that we have been informed that insanity is becoming one of the great menaces of modern American life. Statistics concerning mental unbalance which is a direct commentary upon the nature of man show an increase of forty per cent in the same decade. Investigation is proving that a troubled heart produces heart trouble as well as nervous and mental trouble.

The troubled heart was always a spiritual disease in man. Job said, "man is born unto trouble, as the sparks fly upward." No one is without his troubles and his problems. Well do a minister and a doctor know that. Only this week, a home which had formerly appeared to be about ideal was revealed as one in which there were several deep-seated problems troubling the hearts and heads of that household. This is representative of us all. Even the hearts of the disciples were troubled as they listened to the teaching of Jesus. In the very presence of the great Healer and the Eternal One who manifested the quiet strength of Deity these men were not exempt from this universal human disease. Somehow, as we look about into the faces of men, today, reading the deepening lines, the thinning lips and the wavering eye, the conviction comes upon us that the problems of life are weighing heavier upon the hearts of men than they formerly did. Perhaps that observation is due only to increasing maturity on our own part, but we cannot altogether shake the feeling that we are in an unusual time.

Problems ordinarily are a part of the zest of life.

They are the means of the formation of character through trials. Only the man who struggles with mental and moral enigmas and solves them grows in independence of intellect and moral fiber. Normally we should accept the problems of life as a part of our personal growth, just as a plant must brave the winds and the parasites and the hostile environment in which it grows, or a muscle must tense and relax under the pressure of a difficult task in order to grow strong. Problems are often revelatory of one's nature. The weak and cowardly soul is soon discovered in the presence of a great difficulty. There are some men who breathe freer and rise to undreamed of heights of accomplishment in the presence of danger and difficulty. There are others who, like cravens lowering, creep away and leave the struggle. It is the testing which reveals the difference between the two. Had it not been for the problems facing the apostolic group we might never have received from the lips of Jesus this beautiful and oft quoted chapter in the Bible from which innumerable myriads of men have drawn strength for their personal trials. It is said that when Sir Walter Scott was dying, he asked his attendant to read to him. Glancing at the many books at hand, he asked, "From what?" Scott replied, "Need you ask? There is but one." Then the friend picked up a well-worn Bible and it opened at the fourteenth chapter of John, which he read. "That's it," said the dying author. "There is nothing like that."

I. The Cause of a Troubled Heart.

Just as there are causes for heart trouble, there are also causes of the troubled heart. Modern science has diagnosed many of these troubles of the heart. The human body is nourished and kept alive by the blood. The heart sends this blood through the lungs, where the oxygen we breathe is absorbed by it and then pumps it through an intricate circulatory system to every nerve, muscle and organ in the body. When the heart ceases to function and the blood fails to reach and feed the body, death commences. From the mechanical viewpoint there are less than half a dozen ways in which the heart fails. The muscle itself may break down under this load and lose its power to push the blood through its arteries. This is called myocarditis. Endocarditis is a disturbance of the interior or lining of the heart. The valves may become clogged and fail to act. It is a common occurrence to have in these valves a leakage, sometimes slight, sometimes of more importance. This is the cause of heart murmur. Coronary thrombosis is a damming up of the arteries which feed the heart and which makes it impossible to force the blood through. Tiny clots, forming in the circulatory system, become detached and catch in the coronary or heart artery and cause such a stoppage. The pain which accompanies this condition is known as angina pectoris. Then there are other diseases, like the hardening of the arteries and high blood pressure, which place additional burdens upon the heart. Other diseases, if severe, will weaken the heart muscles by poison induced by them.

What are the causes of a troubled heart? We can put our finger upon three. First, there is the presence of evil in the world which all of us experience. Second, there is unbelief in the promise of God in Christ. Third, there is the lack of understanding.

The disciples faced evils which are similar to those which we must all experience. In this intimate conversation with Jesus they had been instructed by His example that instead of being masters they were to be servants, to wash one another's feet. That troubled them. It was contrary to their expectations. Again, Jesus had recently told them that one of this group would betray Him. They were amazed and they questioned among themselves as to who it was that could do such a dastardly act. Then Jesus singled out Peter and announced that he would deny Him. The startled group considered that if Peter could do this then surely nothing was beyond the possibility of human nature. To cap the climax, Jesus announced that He was going away from them. It was a perplexed, anxious, troubled group to whom He then spoke the words, "Let not your hearts be troubled."

We, too, are faced with evil personified in individuals, as it is brought directly into contact with our lives, and we have been troubled by it. In one of the Psalms the writer says that when he saw the prosperity of the wicked his heart failed him. That has been the condition of many men. What kind of world is this

The Troubled Heart

in which evil men prosper? Then there is the problem of illness, one of the most common causes of the troubled heart. Some righteous souls have been harassed by afflictions most difficult to bear. In fact, separation by death from those whom they have loved often comes as a result of illness. Their hearts are broken and troubled. Some individuals never recover in their affectional functions from separations like that in a family. We may add insecurity to the list. People fret about what the morrow shall bring forth because there is no means of assurance that some form of evil may not be awaiting them. Recently, in a brief conference of ministers, I sat with a man on a sub-committee writing a doctrinal statement. When we were attempting to express the practicability of Christianity, he stood tense in a meditative mood, remembering something that had happened in his life. Then he said, "It must be practicable. We must pray for the forgiveness of our enemies. I pray that prayer every night before I retire and it means the forgiveness of one who made the difference in my life between being independent of and dependent upon what I earn for a livelihood." Insecurity made it hard even for that minister to forgive. Insecurity drives men to fear. There is also misfortune as it comes in what we call an act of God, which may be accident, fire, or material loss, and it is sufficient to trouble our hearts. All this may be called evil, personal and cosmic evil as it operates in the world.

A second cause for the troubled heart is unbelief, lack of faith in the promise and care of God. Jesus said to His disciples, "Ye believe in God, believe also in me." One of the best illustrations of the Trinity is time. The future is like God. It is unknown, unrevealed, infinite in extent. The present is like the revelation of God in Christ. It is always here. It is the future unveiling itself. It is the future becoming real. That is the purpose of Jesus. He made God known to us. The past is like the function of the Holy Spirit. It illumines the present. Our knowledge of history helps us to understand our present day. Thus it is with the Spirit. He speaks of Christ and takes things of Christ and makes them known unto us. Now, if a man believes in God and trusts Him, he believes in the future, for obviously the future is God ever entering into the present and going into the past. Thus he who has his confidence in God finds life just as secure as God is. He is identified with God. We have said that Jesus is the full declaration of God. He would not let men go hungry, as was witnessed by His feeding the multitudes who had listened to Him teach in the wilderness. He would not permit men to be ill for He healed all who came to Him. Moreover, He constantly rebuked men for their feeling of insecurity, assuring them that the Heavenly Father would take care of them. Now, if Jesus was the declaration of God, then we may reverse that saying and quote, "If ye believe in me, believe also in God." Thus faith is the great antidote for the troubled heart and lack of faith is the distinct cause of the troubled heart. Says the Bible definition, "Faith is the substance of things hoped for, the evidence of things not seen." Believe that your future is in the hands of God and that God is like Jesus.

The Troubled Heart

The third cause of the troubled heart is the lack of understanding. When Jesus said these words, "Let not your heart be troubled ... I go to prepare a place for you and I will come again and receive you unto myself; that where I am, there ye may be also," Thomas said, "We know not whither thou goest; and how can we know the way?" These three words, "We know not," describe the condition of the troubled disciples. They simply did not understand what was taking place. Jesus had clearly told them before this time, but their eyes were not opened. Three times, at Paneas, when Peter had pronounced Him the Son of God, at the transfiguration, and beyond Jordan during His Perean ministry, Jesus had said that He must suffer many things of the Pharisees and be put to death by the Gentiles, but their reaction was summarized in the words of Peter, "Far be this from thee." They had listened to Him tell of the spiritual nature of His mission, of the necessity of His death, even of His coming resurrection, but they did not understand, and when the events began to come to pass before their eyes they were troubled in heart and mind. Their condition was like the condition of multitudes of people caught in the meshes of fear because of the things which are taking place in the world, which if they but had eyes to read and a heart to understand what the Scripture says, they would find that God has foretold in great detail, and would also understand that God will take care of them even in the midst of these things. It is the lack of knowledge of the plan of God which makes the chastening and suffering permitted by God the cause of a troubled heart.

II. The Condition of a Troubled Heart.

Recall once more that the heart represents the complete nature of man. When one's heart is troubled it thus affects his complete personality. This is manifested in the attitudes of mind which are so common, such as fearfulness, worry, and anxiety. Jesus said, "Let not your heart be troubled, neither let it be afraid." A fearful heart is usually the evidence of wrong-doing. We think of the old man Eli, who had not restrained his sons in their evil doings, who had not opposed their desire to take the Ark of God illegally into the battle, and who now sat by the wayside watching for the runner who would bring him news of the battle, for his heart trembled for the Ark of God. He was fearful. We think again of Joseph's brethren who had sold him into Egypt and years later had come to buy grain during the time of famine. After leaving Joseph at the first purchase of grain they were on their way back to Canaan when one of them opened his sack of grain and found his money returned therein. We read that their heart failed them. They were afraid because of the evil they had done.

On the other hand, a heart which is established in God will not be afraid. This is the meaning of the twenty-third Psalm. When the soul has accepted the shepherding care of the Lord he may say, "I will not be afraid though I walk through the valley of the shadow of death . . . goodness and mercy shall follow me all the days of my life and I will dwell in the house of the Lord forever." Notable is it that the fearful are excluded from heaven. They are classed with unbelievers, murderers and other sinners as being shut out from the eternal city. Such individuals are not excluded because of their fear, but because fearfulness reveals the presence of sinful unbelief in their heart. The soul of a mature man may be as fearless as that of a youth. We recall the poem quoted in a letter by John C. Stam to his parents when the events were culminating which ended in a martyrdom of himself and Betty his wife by Chinese Communists. Said he:

>"Afraid? Of what?
> To feel the spirit's glad release?
> To pass from pain to perfect peace,
> The strife and strain of life to cease?
>   Afraid—of that?
>
> "Afraid? Of what?
> Afraid to see the Saviour's face,
> To hear His welcome, and to trace
> The glory gleam from wounds of grace?
>   Afraid—of that?
>
> "Afraid? Of what?
> A flash, a crash, a pierced heart;
> Darkness, light, O heaven's art!
> A wound of His a counterpart!
>   Afraid—of that?
>
> "Afraid? Of what?
> To do by death what life could not—

> *Baptise with blood a stony plot,*
> *Till souls shall blossom from the spot?*
> *Afraid—of that?"*

Another attitude is that of worry or anxiety of mind. It would be difficult to distinguish between the two. Jesus' words as translated by the revisers may be quoted, "Be not anxious for your life . . . be not anxious for tomorrow, for the morrow shall take thought for the things of itself. Sufficient unto the day is the evil thereof." Jesus taught that if men would seek first the kingdom of God and His righteousness that all these things would be added unto them. The things included food and raiment and health. He proclaimed a Divine provision made for man and the connection of this provision with righteousness. We cannot help but feel that wherein famine and terrible depression and extraordinary catastrophes occur, they are connected with man's lack of righteousness. If this is true, then the converse is true, that if man obeys God's law he would receive these material benefits. Jesus said to His disciples, "If ye love me keep my commandments," and "If ye ask anything in my name, I will do it." Thus, worry is a result of pride and self-sufficiency rather than dependence upon God. It is quite remarkable how little starvation there is in the world in proportion to the amount of worry over starvation.

There is a harmony between the Pauline command to be anxious in nothing and his own reasonable concern for the progress of the churches, for the salvation of souls and for the safety of those committed to his care, such as in the shipwreck journey, but Paul knew nothing of fretful anxiety. Men would have fewer sleepless nights were it not for their anxiety of soul. Remember that "He giveth his beloved sleep." Such fear, worry and discouragement reveals a troubled heart.

Actions also manifest a condition of the troubled heart. A constant condition such as we have described is a direct cause of the distraction of mind which results in suicide. When we think of the many brilliant and otherwise normal people who have taken their lives, we know that it has not come from some philosophy of life but from a temporary lack of balance produced by a troubled heart. The number of such conclusions to life's problems is increasing. Another action manifesting a troubled heart is irritability of temper and ebullitions of wrath. We think of some who speak quickly and cuttingly to friends and loved ones without meaning so to do and without desiring to hurt simply because the heart is troubled over illness, evil or misfortune. Again there are other multitudes continuing in a neurotic condition caused by the body acting sympathetically with the mind. Worry thus may be manifested in all manner of disorders of body whether digestive, skin or blood diseases. These are incurable as long as the mental or the heart cause remains.

Contrast this with the untroubled heart of Jesus. In the midst of hostility from the Pharisees and the ruling powers, of poverty so that He had not a place to lay His head, of insecurity so that He foretold His own death and of disappointment in those who followed Him, He retained perfect peace, calmness and self-control.

There was an eternity in the heart of Jesus and it was there by faith. He will ever stand for us as the great example of an untroubled heart. Then there is Paul, the greatest of all Christians, who likewise kept himself under so as to be unmoved by the changing conditions of life. This is a quality of life which is promised to believers, and while it is absent from them they have not attained to their full heritage in Christ.

III. THE CURE FOR A TROUBLED HEART.

Jesus presented the cure for this condition in His words to His disciples on this occasion. He presented the Christian view of God and the world, a philosophy. He said, "Believe in God. Believe in me. Believe that I am the Way, the Truth and the Life. Believe in prayer. Believe in the power of God to perform miracles in this world. Believe in the presence of the Holy Spirit." In other words, Jesus declared that God is in His heaven and is still sovereign over the world, that there is a plan to this life, that whatever Jesus did had been done by God Himself, that there is a purpose to suffering and Jesus' death had a real meaning, that there is a provision for Divine power in human life, and that men should pray and should expect to do great works. If we take this Christian view of the world we may have the brightness of Jesus' outlook even in the midst of dark conditions that trouble us. Browning expressed that when he wrote "Pippa Passes." The little factory girl who received a holiday went along singing into the homes of discouraged and saddened men her simple song, "God's in His heaven and all's right with

The Troubled Heart 145

the world." The song brought new life and hope to those who heard it. The Christian philosophy does not state that all is right with the world, but it does tell us that there is a sovereign God Who controls the human affairs of every-day life and thus there is a brightness behind all of the shadows. But this Christian view as a philosophy is meaningless unless it becomes my view and I live according to it. It is Christ or nothing and hence I, as an individual, must trust my all to Christ if my troubled heart is to be cured.

To these disciples Jesus said, "I am the way . . . no man cometh unto the Father but by me." Christianity has been known as *"The* Way." This title was given to it as early as the persecutions of Saul when he went to Damascus to apprehend the men of "this way." They were the men who believed in the Deity of Christ and His power as Saviour. Thus it is that Christ declared that the Christian way to God is through Him. When Philip said, "Shew us the Father and it sufficeth us," Jesus affirmed that the Father dwelled in Him and he who had seen Him had seen the Father. Then He went on to say that whosoever believeth on Him should do greater works than He did because He went unto the Father. The Christian way of life must be continued by Christ dwelling in His present body, which is the Church, and that Church performing the works of Jesus in this present world.

Moreover, Jesus affirmed that the troubled heart may be cured by the Christian life. "I am the life . . . I will pray the Father and He will send you the Comforter." The Comforter is none other than the Spirit of truth, or the Holy Spirit. That Holy Spirit is the full dynamic of the Christian life. He speaks of the things of Christ. He reveals God unto men. He empowers them for great works. He brings truth to their remembrance and He implants a love of the Father and the Son in the human heart. He is called "The Paraclete," that is, the source of all comfort, of encouragement, of help, of life itself. He presents a supernatural power which will keep men from having a troubled heart. If Jesus were here with you, if He walked with you, and talked with you about your problems, if He took your hand in His and looked reassuringly in your eyes, would you be afraid or would you worry? No. Well, He is here. He said, "I will not leave you comfortless: I will come to you. Yet a little while and the world seeth me no more; but ye see me: because I live ye shall live also." Christ in the Spirit is present with us in life. Through Him we may be enabled to face all things. Thus Jesus concluded His words concerning the troubled soul, "Peace I leave with you: my peace I give unto you: not as the world giveth give I unto you. Let not your heart be troubled, neither let it be afraid."

Three days later the disciples were gathered in the upper room behind closed doors, discussing the events which had occurred since Jesus was crucified, and were troubled in heart. Suddenly He stood in the midst of them and said, "Peace be unto you. Why are ye troubled and why do thoughts arise in your hearts? Behold my hands and my feet, that it is myself. Jesus' first question after His resurrection was a rebuke of those whose hearts were troubled. If He were to face

The Troubled Heart

us who have worried and fretted and feared, who failed to commit ourselves to His loving care, His words would be the same, "Why are ye troubled? Why do you not believe in me and understand that I know what is for your own good and that I will take care of you?" If you do believe in Jesus, then let not your heart be troubled neither let it be afraid.

Wipf and Stock Publishers
199 W 8th Ave, Suite 3
Eugene, OR 97401

These Religious Affections
By Ockenga, Harold John and Rosell, Garth M.
Copyright©1937 by Ockenga, Harold John
ISBN 13: 978-1-5326-1736-2
Publication date 1/25/2017
Previously published by Zondervan, 1937

The Loving Heart

perfection or happiness of the ego or self and that all virtue consists in the pursuit of self interest. It has been defined as "the course of action which selects as its end the greatest attainable surplus of pleasure over pain for the agent, pleasures being valued in proportion to their pleasantness." Altruism has been defined as "the instinct and emotion which prompts to action on behalf of others, together with the action thus prompted." Every man is egoistic. George Eliot says in *Daniel Deronda*, "Who has been quite free from egoistic escapes of the imagination picturing desirable consequences on his own future in the presence of another's misfortune, sorrow or death?" No man is free from egoism. It is as fundamental a precept, however, that men must be altruistic. In the kind of world in which we live it seems inevitable that what is for the happiness of the majority does not promote the happiness of the minority. If a person belongs to the majority and his interests are identified with the interests of the majority, it is a simple matter to have him act for the greatest possible good of the greatest number, but when he belongs to the minority and his happiness does not lie in the same channel of interest as that of the majority, how is it possible to get such an individual to promote the happiness of the majority at his personal expense? This is the great problem of social theories.

Three classical answers have been given to this problem as to how we should get identity of interest. The first was advanced by Adam Smith and is called the fusion of interests. This states that the interests of men are fused by sympathy. The happy man is unhappy to see another man unhappy. Sympathy causes the wealthy man to give food to the poor in order to relieve his own distress in seeing them in distress. This is still selfish. It might be called the drive of the self in works of kindness, but by means of this selfishness the interests of the majority and the minority are fused in one and all work for the greatest good of the greatest number. A second answer to the problem is that the interests of men are naturally identified. This states that man knows what is for his own interest and that his good is the good of the group. The interests of men are one and indivisible. It is as if an invisible hand drew all individual efforts into one and by each promoting his own happiness the happiness of all results. This has been know as laissez-faire and has been the doctrine of economics and ethics until recent times. The third answer is that the interests of men must be artificially identified. This implies the assumption that some must be restrained for the good of all. The restraining force is law or public opinion. Rewards and punishments added to certain actions bring the greatest happiness of the individual into alignment with the greatest happiness of society. Simply stated it is: to steal and to suffer the punishment of a fine is productive of less happiness for the individual than the policy of honesty. Thus the individual works for the good of all because of law. Were altruism or the willingness of men to act in behalf of others effectually established in the earth, it would mean the advent of the kingdom of God. Thus we may see why radical philosophers have dealt with this problem as the fundamental means of establishing their Utopia. If the words of Jesus were fulfilled as they are stated in our text, the change ushered into the world would be as great as any which these radical philosophers advocate.

If, therefore, in social theory we substitute religion for revolution it may well be that we have as radical a force for the changing of the world as is inherent in, let us say, Marxist philosophy. The Christian religion proclaims that the creation of loving hearts in men will accomplish what the philosophers desire without the violence or the legislative compulsion which they advocate. The Christian religion deals with society in the form of the individual who, being changed from within, becomes the unit for revolutionizing society. Hence religious affections, which constitute true Christianity, are of supreme importance to the world. Let us turn our attention to the question, How may religion develop the loving heart?

I. ALTRUISM IS A HEART RELIGION REQUIRED BY GOD.

The Bible reveals perfect unity in its teaching concerning the Divine requirement of love. Let us begin with Paul. He said: "Owe no man anything but to love one another, for he that loveth another hath fulfilled the law. For this, thou shalt not commit adultery, thou shalt not kill, thou shalt not steal, thou shalt not bear false witness, thou shalt not covet; and if there be any other commandment, it is briefly comprehended in this saying, thou shalt love thy neighbor as thyself. Love worketh no ill to his neighbor, therefore love is the fulfilling of the law." Some have accused Paul of teaching antinomianism, which is, complete freedom from the law for one who is saved by faith. Paul does emphasize that no man can be saved by obeying the law of Moses, but he never repudiates the obligation of that law. He simply expresses its obligations under the word "love," for love is the fulfilling of the law. This passage can leave no doubt in the mind concerning the attitude of life expected by Paul from the believer.

Jesus' teaching confirms this. During the last week of His life Jesus was questioned by a lawyer who asked, "Master, which is the great commandment in the law?" Jesus answered, "Thou shalt love the Lord thy God with all thy heart, and with all thy soul, and with all thy mind. This is the first and great commandment and the second is like unto it, thou shalt love thy neighbor as thyself. On these two commandments hang all the laws and the prophets." Jesus summarized the Mosaic law in two commandments because there were two sections of the law. When Moses came down from the mount after forty days in the presence of God, he carried with him two tablets of stone on which the ten commandments were inscribed. On the first tablet there were four commandments, the first four of the decalogue, which dealt with man's duty toward God. They were, in brief: "Thou shalt have no other gods before me"; "Thou shalt not take unto thee any graven image"; "Thou shalt not take the name of the Lord thy God in vain"; "Remember the Sabbath day to keep it holy." The first commandment given by Jesus summarizes this attitude of man toward God. It is the reverence, adoration and service of a loving heart. The second tablet contained the last six commands of the decalogue, all of which were above quoted in the words of Paul with the exception of the one, "Honor thy father and thy mother." These are social obligations of men. Jesus summarized them in the words, "Thou shalt love thy neighbor as thyself." Paul's statement was merely a quotation of these words.

Some have been led to think that these two commandments were originated by Jesus. But he in turn was merely quoting from the Pentateuch, that is, the writings of Moses. Moses said: "Hear, oh Israel; the Lord our God is one Lord: and thou shalt love the Lord thy God with all thine heart and with all thy soul, and with all thy might." In another part of the Pentateuch Moses wrote, "Thou shalt love thy neighbor as thyself." The requirements of God concerning a heart of love toward Him and toward our fellow men never changed, throughout the sixteen hundred years of the writing of the Bible, and they have not been abrogated to-day.

There is a prominent teaching of our day that a Christian is to love only his brother in the faith and to do good only to the household of faith. This conception is based upon the words of Paul, "Do good unto all men but especially to the household of faith," and the words of John, "We know that we have passed from death unto life because we love the brethren." The fact that the Christian bears a peculiar relationship to the household of faith does not invalidate his obligation to his fellowmen. John makes it clear that he does not use the word brother only from a Christian sense for he adds, "Whoso hateth his brother is a murderer: and ye know that no murderer hath eternal life in him." Thus we may conclude that John, Paul, Jesus and Moses are all in agreement that it is our obligation to love our fellowmen.

This obligation is beautifully illustrated by Jesus in one of His parables. Once a lawyer asked Him, "Master, what shall I do to inherit eternal life?" Jesus replied, "What is written in the law?" The lawyer said, "Thou shalt love the Lord thy God with all thy heart, and with all thy soul, and with all thy strength, and with all thy mind; and thy neighbor as thyself." Jesus said to him, "Thou hast answered right: this do and thou shalt live." But the lawyer responded, "And who is my neighbor?" In reply Jesus told the parable of the Good Samaritan, who, though despised and an outcast, performed a good deed unto a stranger who had been beaten by robbers and left helpless by the roadside, and who had been abandoned by both a Levite and a priest who had passed him. Jesus clearly declared the Samaritan, who took of his time and substance to care for the stranger in mercy, to be a good neighbor. Thus we are sure from the teaching of the Bible that altruism is the heart religion required by God.

II. Altruism of Heart Is Incompatible With Egoism.

Man does not naturally love anyone but himself. This self-love is attributed by psychologists to the instinct of self-preservation. It is manifested in the drive

The Loving Heart 155

of self for prominence, for possessions, for security, for leadership. Anything which opposes this self-love stirs the opposition of the individual. Naturally, man is dominated by this instinct. Some instincts conflict with this self-love, such as the parental instinct. This often calls for self sacrifice and self abnegation, which seem to be quite the opposite of self-love. Heroism and asceticism, although at first they seem to be in conflict with self-love, are fundamentally a form of self gratification. We would not have you believe that self-love is entirely an evil. We believe it to be a duty. The instinct for preservation is God-given. This commandment to love our neighbor as ourselves implies the duty of honoring the dignity of one's own nature and the nobility of the struggle for its development and security. But this can in no sense be considered altruistic and harmonious with love of one's neighbor.

Necessarily, the basic nature of man must be changed. His own well-being and pleasure must be brought into identity with that of his fellows. If the doctrine of fusion of interests is true, sympathy would be sufficient for us. If the doctrine of natural indentification of interests is true then a "hands-off" policy will bring the desired result. But if men's interests must be identified artificially, then only two means remain. The first may be called external sanctions. The second, inner motivation. Sanctions may take the form of regulatory laws the violation of which brings pain, of customs the violation of which bring social disapproval, of reason the transgression of which brings personal discontent, and of force which compels identification and from which there can be no violation. Force is the means used to bring about communist and fascist revolutions in order to identify the interests of humanity and to make all work for the common good. The failure of the use of force rests in the total disregard of the human equation in life. Men may be temporarily forced into conformity but their basic natures have not been changed. They are doing what they do not desire to do because of compulsion. The second means of changing the nature of man is by inner motivation. Now this is the peculiar sphere of religion. Religion alone can change the heart.

Man's selfish nature may be transformed into an unselfish nature only by supernatural regeneration through the power of the Cross of Christ. This is the sphere of Christianity. Its great work lies in the changing of the nature of man. This change comes about by means of love. Christianity is a religion of love. First, there is God's love manifested in the giving of His only begotten Son for our salvation. Then there was the love of Jesus which carried Him to the Cross as our substitute bearing the penalty of sin. Then there is the love of the Trinity as it manifests itself in applying this redemption to the heart of man. It is the realization of the greatness of this love of God expressed in redemption which attracts the heart of man and kindles love within his soul. Augustine said, "One loving heart sets another on fire." If this is true among men it is true to a greater extent in the relationship between God and man. The experience of the love of God produces a fundamental altruism in human life.

*"Love took up the harp of life,
And smote on all the chords with might;
Smote the chord of self, that, trembling,
Passed in music out of sight."*

III. ALTRUISM MAY BE DISCOVERED IN THE HEART RELATIONSHIP TO GOD.

The New Testament mentions many times the phrase, "The love of God." It speaks of this love as dwelling in the heart, as an affection in which the believer keeps himself and as an object toward which men's hearts are directed. It also seems to be a state of blessing bestowed upon the believer as is evident from the apostolic benediction, "The love of God be with you." This love of God is of two kinds. It is an affection for God and an affection of God, that is, the phrase may be translated with a subjective or an objective genitive.

The affection for God is planted in the heart of the believer after his justification in a way that it could never have been before this event. Paul said, "Therefore, being justified by faith we have peace with God through our Lord Jesus Christ . . . because the love of God is shed abroad in our hearts by the Holy Ghost which is given unto us." The fervent love of God is awakened and sustained in the believer by the presence of the Third Person of the Trinity, the Comforter. This love may be of the same quality as that experienced in the nature of the Trinity itself between the various centers of consciousness. It may become so overwhelming that it is justly typified by the bride's experience in Canticles when she cried, "I am sick of love." According to John, our love for Him becomes more crystallized and definite when we realize how great is His love to us. He said, "In this was manifested the love of God toward us, because that God sent His only begotten Son into the world, that we might live through him. Herein is love, not that we love God, but that He loved us and sent his Son to be the propitiation for our sins." With knowledge that we possess eternal life comes the resultant passion toward God of heart, soul and mind, man's full nature. All the testings which life presents never affect that love, for as Moses said, "The Lord your God proveth you, to know whether ye love the Lord your God with all your heart and with all your soul."

The affection of God is the quality of love which God manifests toward humanity in general, but particularly for those who are the objects of redemption. Generally this is manifested by benevolence unto all men in His acts of kindness, goodness and mercy. If the love of God is placed in the human heart it is only natural that those who experience it should manifest it toward their fellowmen. John said, "Behold what manner of love the Father hath bestowed upon us." It is the same manner of love as that which we are to manifest unto others. There is no other source for such a life as that designated by "the more excellent way," and described in the thirteenth chapter of I Corinthians, than the love which God hath bestowed upon us. Listen to it, "Though I speak with the tongues of men and of angels and have not love I am become as sounding brass, or a tinkling cymbal, and though I have the gift of prophecy, and understand all mysteries, and have all knowledge; and though I have all faith so that I could remove mountains, and have not love, I am nothing; and though I bestow all my goods to feed the poor and though I give my body to be burned and have not love, it profiteth me nothing. Love suffereth long, and is kind; love envieth not; love vaunteth not itself, is not puffed up, doth not behave itself unseemly, seeketh not her own, is not easily provoked, thinketh no evil; rejoiceth not in iniquity, but rejoiceth in the truth; beareth all things, believeth all things, hopeth all things, endureth all things." That quality of love is received by the supernatural gift of the love of God.

Altruism thus may become a normal virtue of the human personality through the Christian religion. It will manifest God expressing Himself in His children. "What manner of love hath the Father bestowed upon us that we should be called the sons of God." We are sons because our egoistic natures, selfish and individualistic, are changed into loving, altruistic personalities.

When the love of God abideth in us all unsocial and anti-social tendencies are overcome by the loving heart. Insecurities, frustrations and disappointments are trusted to Him and fear, which is the dominant motive in the drive of self, is cast out, for: "God is love: and he that dwelleth in love dwelleth in God, and God in him. Herein is our love made perfect that we may have boldness in the day of judgment: because as he is, so are we in this world: There is no fear in love because perfect love casteth out fear."

PRINTED IN THE UNITED STATES OF AMERICA

www.ingramcontent.com/pod-product-compliance
Lightning Source LLC
Chambersburg PA
CBHW071508150426
43191CB00009B/1444